Cambridge Opera Handbooks

Vincenzo Bellini
Norma

Published titles

Ludwig van Beethoven: *Fidelio* by Paul Robinson
Vincenzo Bellini: *Norma* by David Kimbell
Alban Berg: *Lulu* by Douglas Jarman
Alban Berg: *Wozzeck* by Douglas Jarman
Hector Berlioz: *Les Troyens* by Ian Kemp
Georges Bizet: *Carmen* by Susan McClary
Benjamin Britten: *Billy Budd* by Mervyn Cooke and Philip Reed
Benjamin Britten: *Death in Venice* by Donald Mitchell
Benjamin Britten: *Peter Grimes* by Philip Brett
Benjamin Britten: *The Turn of the Screw* by Patricia Howard
Claude Debussy: *Pelléas et Mélisande* by Roger Nichols and Richard Langham Smith
C. W. von Gluck: *Orfeo* by Patricia Howard
Leoš Janáček: *Kát'a Kabanová* by John Tyrrell
Claudio Monteverdi: *Orfeo* by John Whenham
W. A. Mozart: *La clemenza di Tito* by John Rice
W. A. Mozart: *Così fan tutte* by Bruce Alan Brown
W. A. Mozart: *Don Giovanni* by Julian Rushton
W. A. Mozart: *Die Entführung aus dem Serail* by Thomas Bauman
W. A. Mozart: *Idomeneo* by Julian Rushton
W. A. Mozart: *Le nozze di Figaro* by Tim Carter
W. A. Mozart: *Die Zauberflöte* by Peter Branscombe
Giacomo Puccini: *La Bohème* by Arthur Groos and Roger Parker
Giacomo Puccini: *Tosca* by Mosco Carner
Richard Strauss: *Arabella* by Kenneth Birkin
Richard Strauss: *Elektra* by Derrick Puffett
Richard Strauss: *Der Rosenkavalier* by Alan Jefferson
Richard Strauss: *Salome* by Derrick Puffett
Igor Stravinsky: *The Rake's Progress* by Paul Griffiths
Giuseppe Verdi: *Falstaff* by James A. Hepokoski
Giuseppe Verdi: *Otello* by James A. Hepokoski
Richard Wagner: *Die Meistersinger von Nürnberg* by John Warrack
Richard Wagner: *Parsifal* by Lucy Beckett
Kurt Weill: *The Threepenny Opera* by Stephen Hinton

Vincenzo Bellini
Norma

DAVID KIMBELL

Professor of Music
University of Edinburgh

PUBLISHED BY THE PRESS SYNDICATE OF THE UNIVERSITY OF CAMBRIDGE
The Pitt Building, Trumpington Street, Cambridge CB2 1RP, United Kingdom

CAMBRIDGE UNIVERSITY PRESS
The Edinburgh Building, Cambridge CB2 2RU, United Kingdom
40 West 20th Street, New York, NY 10011-4211, USA
10 Stamford Road, Oakleigh, Melbourne 3166, Australia

First published 1998

Printed in the United Kingdom at the University Press, Cambridge

Typeset in Times NR (MT) 10 on 12.25pt in QuarkXPress™ [SE]

A catalogue record for this book is available from the British Library

Library of Congress cataloguing in publication data

Kimbell, David R. B.
Vincenzo Bellini: *Norma* / David Kimbell.
p. cm. – (Cambridge opera handbooks)
Includes bibliographical references and index.
ISBN 0 521 48036 1 (hardback). – ISBN 0 521 48514 2 (paperback)
1. Bellini, Vincenzo, 1801–1835. Norma. I. Title. II. Series.
ML410.B44K56 1998
782.1 – dc21 97-32615 CIP

ISBN 0 521 48036 1 (hardback)
ISBN 0 521 48514 2 (paperback)

Contents

Plates

Plates 1, 2 and 5 are reproduced with permission of the Museo Teatrale alla Scala, Milan; plate 3 with permission of the Accademia Musicale Chigiana, Siena; plate 4 with permission of Scottish Opera, Glasgow.

General preface

This is a series of studies of individual operas, written for the serious opera-goer or record-collector as well as the student or scholar. Each volume has three main concerns. The first is historical: to describe the genesis of the work, its sources or its relation to literary proto-types, the collaboration between librettist and composer, and the first performance and subsequent stage history. The history is itself a record of changing attitudes towards the work, and an index of general changes of taste. The second is analytical and it is grounded in a very full synopsis which considers the opera as a structure of musical and dramatic effects. In most volumes there is also a musical analysis of a section of the score, showing how the music serves or makes the drama. The analysis, like the history, naturally raises questions of interpretation, and the third concern of each volume is to show how critical writing about an opera, like production and performance, can direct or distort appreciation of its structural elements. Some conflict of interpretation is an inevitable part of this account; editors of the handbooks reflect this – by citing classic statements, by commissioning new essays, by taking up their own critical position. A final section gives a select bibliography and guides to other sources.

For Susi, Sergio and Sara

Preface

The purposes of this book are straightforward: to provide a biographical and cultural context for Bellini's *Norma*, to examine its artistic qualities, and to suggest something of the impression it has made on our imaginations and sensibilities in the 165 years since it was first produced in Milan in December 1831. From time to time I have felt entitled to open up my discussion a little to embrace Bellini's work more generally, particularly in presenting some of the critical reactions to his music. For Bellini's career was short; his reputation rests entirely upon his ten operas; and *Norma*, by common consent his finest achievement, represents his genius more comprehensively than is usually the case with any single work by an operatic composer.

I should perhaps make it clear that the book contains neither analysis nor theory as those terms are currently understood in academic circles. I was tempted (though to tell the truth not very tempted) to invite contributions in those modes. On reflection, however, it seemed that a unity and clarity to match the subject would best be achieved by writing the whole thing myself. Besides, while my indebtedness to other scholars is considerable and will be apparent to the reader, I found too many aspects of *Norma* interested me to wish to let them go. Unless otherwise indicated, all translations are my own.

I am grateful to the University of Edinburgh and particularly to my colleagues in the Faculty of Music for enabling me to take a term's sabbatical leave in 1994. I acknowledge the assistance of Mr Jeremy Upton and his colleagues in the Reid Music Library, University of Edinburgh; the staff of the Music Room of the National Library of Scotland; the British Library; the Museo Civico Belliniano, Catania; the Museo Teatrale alla Scala, Milan; the Biblioteca Comunale Carlo Magnani, Pescia; the Accademia Musicale Chigiana, Siena. And I thank most warmly those who have assisted me with their skills, their knowledge, their advice, their friendly support, their hospitality, and many permutations of all these things: Mr and Mrs Steuart Bedford; Maestro Domenico De Meo; Mr and Mrs David Gwilt; Mrs Jo Leighton; Dr Federica Pedriali; Dr Matteo Sansone and Signora Sansone; Professor Jonathan Usher; Miss Beatrice Wickens; Dr Victoria Cooper at Cambridge University Press; and my wife Ingrid.

The indebtedness most happily recalled is to my daughter and son-in-law, Susi and Sergio Cilea, in whose beautiful Sicilian home most of the groundwork for the book was done, and to my young Sicilian friends Fabio Federico, Guglielmo Magri, Giuseppe and Dora Vinci, thanks to whose kindness I learned to savour the subtle pleasures of life in Catania.

A note on Italian prosody

The standard textbook on Italian versification, on which the following remarks are based, is W. Th. Elwert, *Italienische Metrik*, Munich 1968.

The technical terms used in the description of Italian verse depend upon the number of syllables in the line. Thus *quinari*, *senari*, *settenari*, *ottonari*, *novenari*, *decasillabi*, *endecasillabi*, *dodecasillabi* are, respectively, lines of 5, 6, 7, 8, 9, 10, 11 and 12 syllables. This simple principle is, however, complicated by the fact that lines of Italian verse normally have feminine endings. If a line in fact ends with a strong syllable, or is extended by means of an additional weak syllable, these abnormal circumstances are ignored in counting the syllables but acknowledged in an additional descriptive term, either *tronco* – 'truncated' – or *sdrucciolo* – 'sliding'. The following lyric from the opening of *Norma* thus combines normal *settenari* (lines 2, 4, 5, 6), *settenari sdruccioli* (lines 1, 3, 7), and *settenario tronco* (line 8):

> Ite sul colle, o Druidi,
> Ite a spiar ne' cieli
> Quando il suo disco argenteo
> La nuova luna sveli;
> Ed il primier sorriso
> Del virginal suo viso
> Tre volte annunzi il mistico
> Bronzo sacerdotal.

The 'classic' line of Italian verse is the *endecasillabo*; it forms the basis for the *terza rima* (three-line stanzas) of Dante's *Divina Commedia*, for the sonnets and *canzoni* of Petrarch, and for the *ottava rima* (eight-line stanza) of Ariosto and the epic poets. Verses written entirely in non-rhyming *endecasillabi* are known as *versi sciolti*, the Italian equivalent of blank verse. More loosely, the term *versi sciolti* is often used in an operatic context to mean the kind of verse written for recitative. But that is normally a mixture of *endecasillabi* and *settenari* with the occasional rather casual use of rhyme, and should perhaps more strictly be described as *versi a selva*.

A note on the vocal score

The abbreviation VS used throughout the text refers to the modern vocal score (Ricordi, 1974 reprint, plate no. 41684). References are to page, or to page, system and bar (e.g. VS 81.1.1f. = vocal score, page 81, system 1, bar 1 and following).

1 *The composition of the opera*

Preliminaries

The years 1830 and 1831 marked the climax of Bellini's Italian career: the young Sicilian (he celebrated his thirtieth birthday in November 1831, little more than a month before the premiere of *Norma*) was already the most sought-after composer in Italy, evidently the heir to Rossini, quicker to find a distinctive voice than his slightly older contemporary Donizetti. He had arrived in Milan in April 1827 with an enviable reputation earned both at the Conservatorio and in the opera house in Naples; and in his new home, the centre of the Italian Romantic movement, he had confirmed that reputation with two operas, *Il pirata* (1827) and *La straniera* (1829), that were fast carrying his name over the whole civilized world. In the theatre poet Felice Romani he had found a friend and trusted collaborator who was to be his librettist for all the remaining operas he composed before leaving Italy in 1833.

Bellini spent the first months of 1830 in Venice, composing *I Capuleti e i Montecchi* and supervising its rehearsals and staging. Returning to Milan in April, exhausted and in wretched health, he found the city's theatrical life in a state of some turmoil.

At the time La Scala (and indeed La Fenice in Venice from which Bellini had just returned, so circumstances are unlikely to have taken him completely by surprise) was run by a group called 'Giuseppe Crivelli e Compagni'. Since Bellini had a contract with Crivelli for another Venetian opera, he had some interest in the fortunes of the group, and will have observed, perhaps with concern, that it appeared to be on the point of collapse, and that another triumvirate of enthusiasts was bidding to take over its affairs. Duke Pompeo Litta and his businessmen colleagues, Marietti and Soresi, had signed up a starry ensemble of singers, and were now eager to buy out Crivelli's contract with Bellini, as the composer explained in a letter written at about this time, probably to his uncle Vincenzo Ferlito.

> Duke Litta and the two businessmen Marietti and Soresi, having got into their heads the idea of taking over La Scala, and having for that reason signed up Pasta, Rubini and other celebrated performers, have done their utmost to buy my contract from Crivelli; eventually they got it for a settlement of 1500 francs . . . Then they came to see me, and told me that they had purchased my contract only to release me from Crivelli, and not to buy me and my talents; and so it was their intention to tear up the contract . . . giving me the choice of making different demands, and providing that I should be required to compose the opera either for Venice or for Milan . . . and adding that in the Carnival season I should be unable to compose anything but this opera. Since that was my intention in any case, as I told them when they bought me from Crivelli, I have asked for a fee of 12,000 Austrian lire, the equivalent of two thousand four hundred ducats,[1] and for half the ownership of the printed edition, which, if the opera is a success, will bring me three thousand ducats in all. They have agreed to everything; I have been very lucky over this, because in this way I shall earn virtually twice as much as I was contracted for with Crivelli. (Date and address are missing; Cambi 1943, pp. 251–2)

In the event Litta's hopes of taking over La Scala foundered. He therefore decided to set up his brilliant team of performers and composers for a season in the rival Teatro Carcano; and it was there, during the Carnival of 1830–1, that Donizetti's *Anna Bolena* and Bellini's *La sonnambula* were to have their premieres. Meanwhile Crivelli e Compagni resumed at La Scala and La Fenice. Having lost their original contract with Bellini to Litta's group, they now hastened to engage him for two further operas, one each for Milan and Venice. Thus in a very short space of time in the spring and summer of 1830 Bellini entered into the three contracts that were to occupy him for the entire remainder of his Italian career, producing the three operas *La sonnambula*, *Norma*, and *Beatrice di Tenda*, each with a libretto by Romani, each with Giuditta Pasta in the principal role.

A composer's career in post-Napoleonic Italy

Something must be said about the cultural environment in which Bellini worked. And one had best begin from the fundamental point that Italy as a nation-state did not exist in his time, and that therefore the words 'Italy' and 'Italian', already occurring several times in these opening paragraphs, carried rather different connotations from those they do today.

Metternich's observation, in 1847, that the word 'Italy' was nothing more than 'a geographical expression' was, however notorious it has become, largely true. Catania, Naples and Milan, to name only the Italian cities with which Bellini had most to do, had not formed part of a single political entity since the time of Justinian's Eastern Roman Empire in the sixth century. One of the most enduring frontiers in Europe divided Naples from Rome; it was a frontier which survived even the havoc wrought by the conquering Napoleonic armies in the early years of the century. As a boy in Catania and a student in Naples, Bellini was a subject of the Bourbon monarchs Ferdinand IV and his successor Francesco I, 'Kings of the Two Sicilies', as they were curiously styled. In Milan, the centre of his activities from 1827 to 1833, he was a resident of the capital city of one of the Italian provinces of the Austrian Empire. When he went to produce new operas in Genoa or Parma he was to all intents and purposes going abroad, to the Kingdom of Piedmont-Sardinia and the Duchy of Parma respectively, and he needed his passport.

Nevertheless, Metternich underestimated the potency of the word 'Italy', perhaps because he overlooked the fact that, negligible as its political weight may have been, it had in addition to its geographical significance a very considerable cultural authority. Italy, despite the ubiquitous use of dialect for everyday purposes, had a language and a literature graced by some of the most honoured names in European civilization. It had a music too, a music whose chief adornment historically was the *princeps musicae* himself, Pierluigi da Palestrina. The Neapolitan school of the eighteenth century – Alessandro Scarlatti, Pergolesi, Vinci, and their successors – was still revered in Bellini's time for having shown how poetry and music could be joined together in a way that satisfied all the Age of Reason's aspirations towards expressiveness, sensibility, naturalness and truthfulness in art. The fusion of Italian poetry, Italian music and Italian stagecraft in the art of opera had, since Scarlatti's time, acquired an international cultural prestige which it still enjoyed. Indeed, the European 'conquests' of Rossini, the most brilliant of the younger generation of opera composers, were sometimes compared with those of Napoleon on the battlefield.

In Italy itself, opera had formed an indispensable ingredient of civilized life since the latter part of the seventeenth century; it continued to do so into the twentieth century. But at no time was it cultivated more passionately than during what came to be known as the *risorgimento*, the 'rising-up-again' of the Italian people to nationhood and independence, a movement which extended from the Napoleonic period down to the Unification of Italy in the 1860s, and which therefore embraced the whole of Bellini's career. Even small towns had theatres for opera; the larger ones – Milan, Venice, Rome, Naples – had several. The way they were administered and financed (the greater part of the audiences were box-holders, season-ticket-holders, so to speak, who had their own 'private' accommodation in the theatre) made them, during the season, the centre of a city's social life, a gathering-place for the cultured, intellectual, politically conscious classes.

During the course of the eighteenth century it had come to be widely recognized that opera had an educative mission. As long as that mission was to teach the values of a humane and cosmopolitan civility there was no reason to view it as anything but benign. In the more nationalistic atmosphere of the post-Napoleonic age, however, artists' ideas of what constituted an educative mission were sometimes at odds with the interests of those local potentates on whose support the theatres depended. Opera was becoming politicized; or rather opera would have become politicized were it not for the intervention of the censors. Because of them it was rarely possible for overtly political drama to be staged. What therefore happened was that those questions of politics, nationalism, religion, social ethics, that were of the most urgent concern to the more reflective Italians of the *risorgimento* could be explored only indirectly, in disguise, as a kind of allegory in which the contemporary relevance of the theme had to be read from a drama ostensibly set in a distant place and a remote age.

Between 1825, when he was still a student at the Naples Conservatory, and 1833, when he left Italy for France and England, Bellini composed and produced ten operas. By the standards of the time it was not a large number: in the same period Giovanni Pacini composed nearly twenty, Donizetti not far short of thirty. The operatic life of *risorgimento* Italy, unlike that of today, did not depend on a fixed repertory of established masterpieces in many styles and from many periods. On the contrary, it was an overwhelmingly Italian and an overwhelmingly modern repertory: an opera that survived twenty years was a great rarity; every season new operas were composed in astonishing abundance and produced at theatres all over the peninsula. Some years after Bellini's death, in 1845, the Leipzig *Allgemeine musikalische Zeitung*'s Italian correspondent reported that during the previous eight years 342 new operas had been staged in Italy, and 130 new maestros had made their debut (Verdi and 129 others!).

Composers and librettists could only produce new work at this rate, singers could only learn it and audiences only digest it, on the basis of a flourishing tradition of operatic practice set in a clearly understood social framework. This circumstance gave nineteenth-century Italian opera a musical language and a formal structure that were in many respects deeply conventional; this is as true of a masterpiece like *Norma* as of the most witless hackwork. Of any ten musical and dramatic facts that one might note in the case of *Norma*, seven or eight would be equally true of the most routine production of Bellini's lesser contemporaries. *Norma* is therefore not a unique masterpiece in the way that *Falstaff* or *Die Meistersinger von Nürnberg* or *Pelléas et Mélisande* are; rather it represents the highest of which a particular *type* of opera is capable.

Collaboration with Romani

Virtually all Romani's librettos were based on dramas from the contemporary Parisian theatre. This presupposes that he took the trouble to keep well in touch with theatre life in the French capital; and he will therefore have noticed that on 16 April 1831, *Norma*, a new play by Alexandre Soumet, had had its successful premiere at the Théâtre de l'Odéon. Within a few weeks he and Bellini had agreed that Soumet's play should be the model for their forthcoming La Scala commission. On 20 July Romani reported to Crivelli that he had finished planning the libretto (l'orditura) and was about to set to work writing it (Roccatagliati 1996, p. 100).

Bellini spent the summer months at Moltrasio on Lake Como as a guest of the Turina and Cantù families. By the end of August he was back in Milan, ready to begin work, and on 1 September he wrote to Pasta, who at the time was singing in Paris:

> I now have to apply myself to the opera of which Romani gave me the Introduction [in Cambi 'the plot' [intreccio]] only yesterday. I hope that this subject will prove to be to your taste. Romani believes it will be very effective, and absolutely ideal for your encyclopaedic character, because that's the sort of character Norma has. He will design the scenes in such a way that they bear no resemblance to other subjects, and touch up the characters, and even change them, if that prove necessary to get the best effect. You will have read it already [the play, presumably], and if any thoughts about it occur to you,

do write to me; in the meantime, make sure you get hold of the figurines of the characters as they are performed in Paris, and if you think it a good idea you could even improve them a bit if you feel they are not in the best taste. (Adamo, in Adamo and Lippmann 1981, p. 164, from Lippmann 1977, pp. 283–4)

By 7 September Bellini could report to Giuditta Turina, 'I have almost finished the Sinfonia for the opera and sketched a chorus for the *Introduzione*, and am not displeased with them' (Cambi 1943, p. 281).

Almost nothing is known about the autumn months during which Bellini and Romani worked on the opera. The information that it was finished and ready for rehearsal towards the end of November or the beginning of December comes to us second-hand via Mercadante in a letter to Florimo, the dearest friend of Bellini's student years in Naples. The context of the letter is a request from Florimo to Mercadante to collect autographs of famous musicians for the album of the young Duchess of Noja.

It is already twenty days ago that I sent [the album] to Bellini with a covering letter. He was happy to agree, and I think it will interest you if I repeat one of his paragraphs, which made me laugh heartily. 'On Monday I shall start rehearsing my opera *Norma*, and I believe you will be doing the same.[2] I have made my will, in case they murder me, and remembered to leave you something; in case the same should happen to you, I beg you not to forget me.' I thought that was witty, and I'm sure you will be of the same opinion. (Letter of 12 December 1831, Adamo, in Adamo and Lippmann, 1981, p. 166, from Pastura 1959b, p. 294)

Bellini was a demanding and sometimes difficult composer to work with. Emilia Branca, Romani's wife and biographer and, it must be said, no impartial observer, describes him as so tireless in his insistence on having everything exactly right that 'without undue exaggeration, one could assert that Romani wrote more than three *Normas*, if you want to add together all the variants that we have found, all of them beautiful' (Branca 1882, p. 172).

The demands to which Romani was subjected during the composition of the text were various, and of course they did not all stem from Bellini. As librettist, he was also responsible for dealing with the censorship, and though this was something he was experienced in and probably rather good at, it did in this instance prove irksome, notably on the subject of the Act II war-hymn. Branca's version of the incident is as follows:

Nor did [the censorship] wish to permit the war-hymn in the second act:

Guerra, guerra! Le galliche selve
Quante han quercie producon guerrier, etc.

and still less did it approve of the following lines, where it claimed to perceive the name of Austria instead of that of Rome, and the Imperial eagle instead of the Roman eagle. Here too variants are found in the sketches, corrected by orders from above . . . Bellini was desperate; time was pressing; our poet, who didn't wish to change any more, thanks to his conciliatory manner and the influence he enjoyed with the governing directors of the royal theatres, finally succeeded in foiling the insistent opposition of the censors. (*Ibid.*, pp. 172–3)

The allusion to 'hostile eagles' in Oroveso's Act I aria was also scrutinized with profound suspicion, but ultimately allowed to stand (*ibid.*). On the other hand, still according to Branca, a whole section from the *tempo di mezzo* of Norma's cavatina was removed at the insistence of the censors. (For further details, see the discussion of this movement in Chapter 4.)

Sometimes it was Romani's stubbornness in standing by his own dramatic vision that was the source of the protracted debates. It seems clear, for example, that it was he who insisted – despite the imprecations of the impresario, and despite even Bellini's doubts – that neither act of the opera could be allowed to finish in conventional fashion. Again we depend on Branca for the clearest account of what is supposed to have happened:

The impresario ardently besought the poet to bring back the Druids [at the end of Act I], but since the action did not permit it, Felice Romani, who already in other productions had emancipated himself from the pressures of the stage, and intended to free melodrama entirely from convention, flatly refused, even though he was doubtful of the public's approbation. And he wasn't far wrong, because when the curtain fell, if they didn't whistle . . . at least they were dead silent. Neither did Romani agree with the impresario about the [second act] finale, or with the singers, or with the theatre people. They wanted the funeral pyre on the stage, they wanted the customary grand *aria di forza* for the prima donna. Here too, firm in his resolution and in his views, he let people have their say and went on directly ahead, confident that time would prove him right, as it has done. (*Ibid.*, p. 167)

This time Branca's account is confirmed, in part at least, by Bellini himself who, after a revival of the opera in Bergamo the following summer, acknowledged that Romani had been absolutely correct:

The trio could not have been better performed. They act it well and strongly; it thrilled everyone, and they found it a beautiful finale, even without the *pertichini*, the druids and druidesses and other choruses added simply to make a racket. You were quite right to insist that that is how it should be. (Letter of 24 August 1832, Cambi 1943, p. 320)[3]

Censorship problems and passages where Romani felt he had to insist on having his own way were presumably the exceptional incidents in the weeks of work on *Norma*. Essentially his task was to draft a libretto, the finer details of which would then be hammered out in accordance with the demands of an exceptionally exigent composer. We may of course presume a dialogue: Romani was not a man simply to take instructions, like, say, Verdi's Piave. As Bellini came to compose the first version of this text something will have displeased or dissatisfied him, or created technical or expressive difficulties he was unable or unwilling to solve. Or, in the course of the discussion Romani himself will have had second thoughts. Because composer and poet lived close to one another in Milan and obviously met frequently during these weeks, the evidence for these remarks comes not from letters or other unambiguous documents; it comes from the various layers of their manuscripts, musical and poetic. (See Chapter 4.)

Collaboration with the singers

Scarcely less important than Bellini's relationship with Romani was that with his singers, for no Italian composer of this period could create his operas in a kind of idealistic vacuum, hoping that somehow the right performers would materialize. Operas were written for particular companies, performing in particular theatres during particular seasons. The commercial pressures under which these companies operated meant that their success needed to be immediate. It would have been madness for a composer not to write to his singers' strengths: the particular qualities of their voices, their styles of acting, their taste. An essential stage in the preparation of any opera in the *primo ottocento* was getting to know one's singers.

The minor roles presented no problems, for little or nothing was required in the way of taking account of the performers' idiosyncrasies. In any case Bellini knew them both: Marietta Sacchi, his Clotilde, had taken part in two Bellini premieres, as Adele in *Il pirata* and as Fatima in *Zaira*. His Flavio, Lorenzo Lombardi, also sang in the premiere of *Il pirata* as Itulbo, and Bellini had worked with him again at the Milan premiere of *Bianca e Fernando* (in which he sang Uggero).

It was very different in the case of the other singer with whom Bellini had already worked, his Norma, Giuditta Pasta. She had 'created' the role of Amina in *La sonnambula*, and was to go on to 'create' that of Beatrice di Tenda. But her part in Bellini's life was much more than that of a great artist. She was, in Tintori's words, 'a woman of exquisite sensibility', and since he first met her, probably in the summer of 1828, Bellini had come to regard her as a trusted friend and counsellor. He and Romani used to draw her into their discussions about suitable subjects for new operas: she was involved in the choice of both the abortive *Ernani* in July 1830 and *Beatrice di Tenda* in the autumn of 1832 (Weinstock 1972, pp. 91, 125; Cambi 1943, p. 256), and very likely of *La sonnambula* and *Norma* too. In 1828 she had advised Bellini on the financial arrangements he was making for a prospective visit to London. The respect she inspired enabled her to exert a calming influence on him when the strain of rehearsal stretched his brittle temperament to breaking point (cf. the incident recorded by Branca at the dress rehearsal of *La sonnambula* (Adamo, in Adamo and Lippmann 1981, p. 150)). 'When I begin to speak of that divine woman,' he once told her husband, 'my mind doesn't give me terms to express what I feel' (letter of 28 April 1832, Cambi 1943, p. 312).

Although Pasta was a great singer already in her mid-thirties, *Norma* was to be her debut at *La Scala*. Adamo may speak for the many who had found this

> a surprising fact, which can be explained only by taking account of certain allusions which recur in Bellini's letters, about the hostility of a 'powerful person' towards the celebrated soprano; everything gives us to believe that the person was Duke Carlo Visconti di Modrone, at the time superintendent of the Milanese theatres, and shortly afterwards also the impresario of La Scala . . . Obvious confirmation of the hostility of Modrone with regard to Pasta is the fact that, after he had taken over the management of La Scala, the singer was excluded from it for a further four years. (Adamo, in Adamo and Lippmann 1981, p. 177)

Be that as it may,[4] *Norma* was to be one of the operas with which, for the rest of her career, she was most closely associated, and a number of documents and anecdotes testify to her role in its creation.[5] Her great *sortita*, and specifically its *cantabile* 'Casta Diva', is the subject of a familiar anecdote recorded by Scherillo. Allegedly Pasta at first refused to sing the aria, finding it ill suited to her vocal qualities:

> The maestro used all his powers of persuasion, but with little success. They made a pact: she would keep the piece for a week, going over it again every morning; and if at the end of the seven days she was still averse to performing it, Bellini promised to change it for her. Matters took their inevitable course: 'Casta Diva' was one of the pieces which secured the singer's triumph! (Quoted by Adamo, *ibid.*, p. 166, from Scherillo 1882, p. 84)

Given the state of the autographs of both the score and the libretto, there can be no doubt that 'Casta Diva' was assiduously and long toiled over. That may be felt to provide some circumstantial support to Scherillo's anecdote, as may the gift Pasta subsequently made to Bellini, which had something of the flavour of a peace-offering. On the day of the premiere, she presented him with a richly embroidered parchment lampshade and a posy of artificial flowers made from cloth. The gift was accompanied by a gracious note:

> Permit me to offer you something that was of some comfort to me in the immense nervousness that always torments me when I find myself little fitted to perform your sublime harmonies: this lamp by night and these flowers by day were witnesses to my studies for *Norma*, and no less of the desire I cherish of being always more deserving of your esteem. (Adamo, in Adamo and Lippmann 1981, p. 167, from Pastura 1959b, p. 295)

Pasta's role in the transposition of 'Casta Diva' from G major to F major can only be guessed at. G major, the key of the autograph, is clearly the 'right' key, approached from the previous recitative via a characteristic Neapolitan modulation, left again by the G pivot note of the *banda* that launches the *tempo di mezzo*. But almost all printed editions (Sullivan's Royal Edition is an exception) and manuscript copies are in F, and it seems doubtful whether it was ever performed in G major until Callas did so in 1953 (Weinstock 1972, p. 273). Brauner's conjecture that Pasta sang it in G, but that then, with Bellini's approval, it was transposed for the benefit of the larger number of prima donnas who would be unable to cope with it in the high key (Brauner 1976, p. 116) seems less plausible than the 'tradition' that the transposition was made for Pasta. It is the kind of concession the composer might well have been willing to make if it helped persuade her that the music did suit her voice.

For Bellini was prepared to be indulgent towards the 'divine' Pasta in a way that he was not towards singers in whom he had a less absolute trust. Writing to her husband at the time he was preparing for the Bergamo revival of *Norma*, he remarked

> As far as *Norma* is concerned I shall alter anything that the good Giuditta wishes to have changed; but I shan't write a single new note for any of the other singers . . . whether the music is good or bad, they are always the same rabble of dogs. (Letter of 28 April 1832, Cambi 1943, p. 312)

It is therefore possible, even likely, that certain alternative readings which Bellini later inserted in the autograph score were made in deference to her, either for the Bergamo production or for her debut in London in June 1833, which was also under Bellini's supervision (Lippmann, quoted in Weinstock 1972, p. 429).

The other singers were new to Bellini, though he had worked with Giulia Grisi's elder sister Giuditta. After her Adalgisa in *Norma*, Grisi went on to 'create' the role of Elvira in *I Puritani*, and thus became one of the fabled 'Puritani Quartet' who for years were viewed as the most authoritative exponents of the style of singing demanded by Bellini's operas. The documentation of her relationship with the composer is, however, disappointingly slight. No letters to her seem to have survived, and no anecdote or tradition about their working relationship. All we have are Bellini's comments on her performances, from which it is evident that he regarded her with nothing like the enthusiasm he felt for Pasta; he judged her to be accomplished, certainly, but only within a much narrower range of expression. His most considered observations on Grisi's singing come in a letter to Florimo, giving an account of the failure of a London *Norma* in which she had sung the title role.‘

It was a disappointment for Bellini that Rubini, previously his Gernando, his Gualtiero, his Elvino, and later his Arturo, was not engaged for *Norma*, especially since, in the past, he had not been particularly enamoured of the singing of Domenico Donzelli, whose voice he found 'hard and with a low tessitura' (letter to Florimo, 4 August 1828, Cambi 1943, p. 144). But Donzelli was a distinguished artist, famous for the energy of his singing, and recognizing that other good musicians had wider experience of him than he did himself, Bellini consulted Mercadante. This may have prompted Mercadante to give Donzelli a hint of Bellini's concern. At any rate, in the summer of 1831 there was a cordial, if slightly pompous, exchange of letters between singer and composer.

Donzelli's letter, dated 3 May 1831, was sent from Paris:

I think that it will not be unwelcome to you to have some precise information about my style of singing, on the range and character of my voice, as much to direct your own inspirations, as to make it possible for me to perform them in such a way that they correspond to the effect you desire, which must contribute to the success of your music and to that of my own art. I very much desire to be equal to your demands, because although I do not yet have the pleasure of knowing you, I admire and love your compositions, and I should like to hope that the modest reputation which has assured me of a long career, might now awaken in you the kind of interest that arises for a person who has managed to pass his time and his studies with some profit.

Well then, the range of my voice is about two octaves, from low *c* to top *c*. The chest voice extends up to *g*, and it is in this part of my voice that I can declaim with even force, and sustain the declamation with the full power of the voice. From high *g* to top *c* I can make use of a falsetto which, employed with skill and with power, provides an ornamental resource. I have sufficient agility, but find it considerably easier in descending than in ascending passages. (Adamo, in Adamo and Lippmann 1981, p. 158, quoted from A. Damerini in *Corriere emiliano*, 9 January 1932)

Bellini replied on 7 June:

Sir, your letter has entirely anticipated my wish, which had been to write to you for all the information which you have detailed with such precision about the nature and potential of your voice.

Maestro Mercadante, a close friend of mine, had already given me a fair idea of it, and he also spoke much about your passionate commitment in performing with enthusiasm all music, by whatever composer, which is entrusted to you. So I am already well satisfied *having to compose my opera for a celebrated artist such as yourself*, and also for a man of such estimable sentiments; so I shall torture my brain to make sure that you are as satisfied with me as I am with you. The mainstays of my composition are Donzelli and Pasta alone, for which reason the subject of the opera cannot but be focused on these two artists. (Adamo/Damerini, *ibid.*)

Donzelli's hopes that Bellini might come to take a special interest in him were not to be realized. He was to repeat the role of Pollione in both the Vienna and London premieres (Weinstock 1972, pp. 270–1), but had no further close association with Bellini. It is worth recording the view of Donizetti, who attended several performances during the first run of the opera, that Donzelli was already a bit on the old side for a lover's role (letter of July 1835, quoted in Roccatagliati 1996, p. 90).

If the exchange of letters with Donzelli shows most clearly the working relationship between composer and performer typical of the period, the case of the remaining singer, his Oroveso, Vincenzo

Negrini, shows what might happen when a composer had not done his homework thoroughly (or perhaps Bellini had been simply misled). Oroveso's role is curious for containing both a cavatina and a *sortita*, terms usually synonymous at this period. Both pieces are single-movement arias heavily dependent upon the chorus. Of course, in part this is a function of Oroveso's dramatic role in the opera. But Bellini and Romani had originally envisaged a larger part, more wide-ranging in vocal expression, only to find that Negrini had a weak heart and that the cabaletta in his big Act II *scena* would have to be cancelled for fear of overtaxing him.

The premiere

It has been calculated that rehearsals for *Norma* began on Monday 5 December 1831 (Weinstock 1972, p. 104). Save for the 'Casta Diva' incident we know very little about their progress. Scherillo reports that Bellini was at first reluctant to name the opera after its protagonist, wanting

> to give it a title different from the original French tragedy, and . . . to create a bit of a public stir, *La selva druidica* was suggested, and *La druidessa* and *I druidi*; but none of these titles pleased him, and finally he had to content himself with *Norma* because the impresario could not wait any longer. (Scherillo 1882, pp. 88–9)

On 19 December, La Scala published its *cartellone* for the approaching Carnival Season. It announced that

> The season will open with the *opera seria Norma*, in which roles will be taken by the signore Giuditta Pasta, Giulia Grisi, and Marietta Sacchi and the signori Domenico Donzelli, Vincenzo Negrini, and Lorenzo Lombardi. With the grand ballet entitled *Merope* and the demi-character ballet *I Pazzi per progetto*.[7] (Weinstock 1972, pp. 104–5)

As so often happened at this period, rehearsal time was barely sufficient to get the opera on stage by the appointed day. The death of Crivelli on 16 December, after which Merelli assumed the direction of the company, must have been a distressing and distracting incident that can only have exacerbated this traditional problem (Rosselli 1984, p. 26). Nevertheless, Bellini, who was a shrewdly self-critical artist, can have had little doubt that he had composed his finest opera. He was also accustomed to success; and though he might have felt a little nervous of Modrone's attitude to Pasta, and though he might have imagined the Countess Samoyloff and other enthusiasts for

Pacini or any other supposed rival conspiring to bring about the failure of *Norma*, he must have felt confident that, well cast as it was, it would win the audience's whole-hearted enthusiasm.[8] He was wrong: the opening night of the opera was coolly received, and in his over-wrought emotional state he could not but feel the occasion to have been a 'fiasco'.[9]

The reviews show that Bellini was right to feel that his audience was cool, wrong to speak of the evening, if he did so speak of it, as a fearful débâcle. The *Eco* of 28 December seems to provide a judicious appraisal of the first night:

From a composer like Bellini, from artists like Madame Pasta and Donzelli, one can reasonably anticipate something out of the ordinary; and yet . . . we are obliged to inform our foreign readers [i.e. those outside Milan; those in Milan will have known already], to their no small surprise, that at the end of the first act, not the slightest sign of applause was to be perceived, even if, during the course of the act, justice had been done to the *sinfonia*, the introduction (perhaps a little too long), and the distinguished singing of Madame Pasta and Donzelli. The public, which certainly was expecting to hear the first act close with a grand finale, found itself deluded and was ill-pleased to see the curtain fall after a not very effective trio.

The second act contains some beautiful pieces of music; for example we would mention a duet between Norma and Adalgisa, another between Norma and Pollione, and the finale, which, however, both in the situation and in the music, brings to mind the finale of the first act of Spontini's *La vestale* [he means the second act].

In this act Madame Pasta, Signor Donzelli and Mademoiselle Grisi, and the composer likewise, had less equivocal proof of the public's satisfaction, and at the close were called on stage repeatedly; and we are inwardly convinced that, generally speaking, the whole opera, when it has been heard more often, and when a few evident defects in the performance have gradually disappeared, will finish up by pleasing. (Adamo, in Adamo and Lippmann 1981, p. 179)

By the third performance the singers had settled into their roles, the audiences had the measure of the new opera, and Bellini himself felt able to reflect relatively calmly on what had been an emotionally taxing week. On 31 December he wrote two letters. I quote from that to Giuseppe Ruggieri, a bass singer who had been a fellow pupil in Naples:

I wanted to await the outcome of the first three performances so that I could give you the real news about *Norma*. All in all the opera has created a furore: on the first evening, because the singers were barely able to perform at all the trio that ends the first act (they were so tired), it finished very frigidly indeed; but on the second evening the terzetto was sung a little better and was reasonably well-liked, but still not as much as I believe it should be, because it's a piece that demands a lot of strength, and the singers really do need to be well rested; but still it sufficed, on two evenings, the second and the third, for me to be called for on stage. Then, on all three evenings, the second act created wild enthusiasm, despite a hostile faction, formed with large sums of money poured out by that mad woman who is the protector of another composer,[10] whom you will easily guess, and the effect of the duet between Donzelli and Pasta and the finale is magical, and I confess myself that they are the most beautiful pieces I have yet written; and so on all three evenings I was obliged, at the end of the opera, to show myself a good four times on stage. The pieces that make a cold effect, and which always will do with this company, are the stretta of Donzelli's cavatina, and the duet between him and Grisi . . . That is the news then, which you will find very different from what the newspapers give: they, to distort things, have had money from the purse of that woman; but the theatre is always full, every evening there is complete silence: the applause is unanimous: if these things indicate a fiasco then *Norma* has been a fiasco. (*Ibid.*, p. 180; Cambi 1943, pp. 297–8)

On 5 January 1832 Bellini left Milan for an extended visit to Naples and Sicily. Though he still had some reservations about it, *Norma* had clearly taken; before the end of the season it had enjoyed no fewer than twenty-four performances.

2 *Medea – Velleda – Norma: Romani's sources*

Medea

The tale of Medea is a harrowing one even by the standards of Greek mythology; of its various elements it is the Corinthian episode that has lingered most vividly in the appalled imagination.

Medea, a princess of Colchis, to the east of the Euxine (Black) Sea, was an enchantress and priestess of the moon-goddess Hecate. When Jason came to Colchis in his quest for the Golden Fleece, Medea fell in love with him, employed her magic arts to help him win the Fleece, then sailed with him as he made his escape from the enraged King of Colchis, her father. Their flight to Corinth was accompanied by horrid demonstrations both of her magical powers and of her ruthlessness, notably the murder and dismembering of her brother and the jettisoning of him overboard piece by piece to delay the pursuit of her father's ship (which out of religious duty was bound to gather up the floating limbs to give them proper burial).

Medea bore Jason two sons, but once he was back in civilized Greece, he could not – despite all his vows – be happy to remain the husband of a murderous Asiatic enchantress, and entered into a contract of marriage with Glauce, daughter of the King of Corinth. Maddened with jealousy and contempt for Jason, Medea sent Glauce a poisoned coronet and robe, which killed her by burning away her flesh. Then, to torment Jason further, she put to the sword the two sons she had borne him, before riding away from Corinth in a flying chariot drawn by dragons.

As a depiction of the very darkest potential of the human mind and the destructiveness of uncontrollable passion, the myth has fascinated dramatists throughout the ages. First given its definitive form in Euripides' earliest surviving tragedy, *Medea*, in 431 BC, it was taken up again in classic examples of Latin (Seneca), French (Corneille) and German (Grillparzer) tragedy. Amid a host of operatic workings of the same story, three – Cavalli's *Giasone* (1649), M.-A. Charpentier's *Médée* (1693), Cherubini's *Médée* (1797) – stand among the masterpieces of the genre in their particular time and place. Cherubini's opera, which, in Brahms's words, 'we musicians regard among ourselves as the summit of dramatic music', would have been familiar to both Romani and Bellini since, in translation, it had become a staple of the Italian repertory in the early nineteenth century and remained so until the 1830s. In 1813, the young Romani had himself written a *Medea in Corinto* for Naples. It was the libretto that confirmed his reputation as the most talented theatre-poet in Italy, and set to music by Simone Mayr it proved one of the longest-lived serious operas of its period; in the title-role, originally written for Isabella Colbran, Giuditta Pasta was to enjoy one of her greatest triumphs.

Medea is of course not Norma. But clearly she is the source of several of Norma's most distinctive and theatrical traits. An enchantress and priestess serving the moon-goddess in a remote and mysterious land beyond the bounds of the civilized world, she falls in love with and bears two sons to a prosaic, buccaneering hero from classical Mediterranean territory. When he abandons her for another woman, her humanity is so overwhelmed by passion as to bring her to contemplate the murder of her own children.

Velleda

Viewed from a Mediterranean perspective the lands to the north-west of the civilized ancient world were no less mysterious and terrible than those to the north-east. There, in classical times, lived another woman who has much bearing on our story, a virgin prophetess wielding immense authority among the Bructeri. Tacitus and other authors gave her the name of Velleda. Velleda's role in literary history is far more modest than that of Medea; but in 1809 Chateaubriand transported her to Gaul and made her a central figure in his prose epic, *Les martyrs*. Book IX of *Les martyrs* tells the story of the relationship between Velleda and a Roman officer, Eudore. Except that Eudore is a Christian, Chateaubriand's tale might be described as the story of *Norma* told from a different perspective and, as it were, in the form of an autobiographical novel. And being a novel, it provides a wealth of picturesque and evocative description which evidently fascinated Romani, and encouraged him to pay particular care to the evocation of atmosphere in his libretto.

The following is the story as told in the book – and in so far as it has any bearing on the opera. Eudore is speaking.

(Velleda) was tall; a black tunic, short and sleeveless, scarcely served to veil her nakedness. She carried a golden sickle hanging from a belt of bronze, and she wore a crown made of oak twigs. The whiteness of her arms and complexion, her blue eyes, her red lips, her long fair hair, which floated loose, all declared a daughter of the Gauls, and in their gentleness contrasted with her proud and savage deportment. With a melodious voice she sang terrible words, and her bare breast rose and fell like the foam of the waves . . . The young girl stopped not far from the stone, and clapped her hands three times, calling out the mysterious word: 'Au-gui-l'an-neuf' [the new year of the mistletoe]. In a moment I saw a thousand lights gleaming in the depths of the forest; every tree, so to speak, gave birth to a Gaul.

[After Velleda had attempted to foment rebellion against the Romans] One heard the distant chorus of bards, singing these sombre words as they went away: 'Teutatès will have blood; he has spoken in the Druids' oak. The sacred mistletoe has been cut with a golden sickle on the sixth day of the moon, on the first day of the century. Teutatès will have blood; he has spoken in the Druids' oak.

[One night she appears to Eudore and tells him she is an enchantress] The enchantresses of Gaul . . . have the power of raising tempests and of exorcizing them, of making themselves invisible, of taking the form of different animals.

[Eudore gradually feels himself falling under her spell] In vain I kept myself out of Velleda's sight. I found her everywhere; she used to wait for me all day long in places I could not avoid, and there she spoke to me of her love. It is true, I felt that Velleda would never inspire in me a genuine attachment: for me she lacked that secret charm which gives our life its destiny. But the daughter of Ségenax was young, she was beautiful, passionate, and when burning words came from her lips all my senses were confounded . . .

Some distance from the castle, in one of those forests which the Druids call sacred, a dead tree was visible, its bark peeled off with knives. This phantom-like object was distinguishable by its pale colour in the midst of the dark recesses of the forest. Worshipped under the name of Irminsul, it had become a formidable divinity for those barbarians who, in their joys and sorrows alike, knew only how to invoke Death. Around this idol, a number of oaks whose roots had been watered with human blood, carried Gallic weapons and insignia of war suspended from their arms; the wind stirred them on the branches, and in knocking against one another, they gave out sinister murmurs.

[Once while Eudore is standing by the Irminsul, Velleda suddenly appears] Then approaching me as if she was delirious, she put her hand over my heart. 'Warrior, your heart remains tranquil under the hand of love; but perhaps a throne would make it beat faster. Speak; do you want the Empire?

. . . I shall arm our warriors in secret. Teutatès will favour you and, by my art, I shall compel heaven to grant your wishes.'

[There are more meetings during which Eudore with difficulty resists her charms. She attempts to kill herself by leaping from the cliffs into the sea. Eudore struggles to restrain her. Eventually they become lovers, but] to me my happiness seemed like despair, and anyone who had seen us in the midst of our joy would have taken us for two guilty creatures on whom sentence of death had just been passed. In that moment, I felt myself marked by the stamp of divine reprobation: I doubted the possibility of my salvation and the omnipotence of God's mercy.

[The Romans are met by a horde of Gauls led by Velleda's father, Ségenax] 'Gauls,' he cried, 'I bear witness with these arms of my youth, which I have taken once more from the tree of Irminsul where I had consecrated them, there is the man who has dishonoured my white hair. A Eubage had been following my daughter, who has lost her reason: in the shadows he saw the Roman's crime. The virgin of Sayne has been violated. Avenge your daughters and your wives, avenge the Gauls and your Gods.'

[In the skirmish that follows Ségenax is killed] At this moment a chariot appeared at the far end of the clearing. Leaning over the steeds a dishevelled woman is fanning their ardour, and seems to want to give them wings . . .

'Gauls, cease your fighting. It is I who have caused your ills, I who have killed my father. Do not any longer risk your lives for a wicked daughter. The Roman is innocent. The virgin of Sayne has not been violated at all: she offered herself, she willingly broke her vows. May my death bring peace to my country!'

Then tearing from her forehead her crown of vervain, and taking from her belt her golden sickle, as if she were about to offer a sacrifice to her gods, she said: 'I shall not again sully these vestal's adornments.' Immediately she put the sacred instrument to her throat: the blood spurted out . . .

If the resemblances between this story and that of Medea are less than obvious, it is because the parallels are, as it were, reversals rather than replications. Cultures clash not within the frontiers of the civilized world but beyond them; the greater part of the story takes place before the Greek/Roman man-of-action hero succumbs to the enchantress's charms, and even when he does she bears him no children; catharsis comes not with the slaughter of the innocent but with the self-sacrifice of the guilty.

The lure of the North

Until about 1815 the majority of Italian serious operas had been based on stories taken from classical history and mythology. When librettists wished to get away from that traditional repertory of themes, they did so by turning to the classics of their own literature:

the epic poems of Ariosto and Tasso; the tales of Boccaccio and Boiardo. Not only were the names and adventures of the principal characters likely to be familiar to audiences; the language was normally permeated by well-loved imagery rooted in Mediterranean geography, in classical history and mythology. Audiences were entirely at home in the imaginative world in which the opera was located.

In *Norma*, the Roman pro-consul Pollione provides a link with this world; sometimes he reminds us of it, as in his dream narrative, 'Meco all'altar di Venere'. But the opera as a whole is very differently located, amid the impenetrable forests of northern Europe, bathed in moonlight rather than sun-drenched; its priests are druids and eubages, its gods those of Germanic mythology.

Romani, who was for some years a classical scholar by profession, did not drift into northern Europe as a mere dilettante. The most substantial and enduring achievement of his years as a teacher at Genoa University was a dictionary of mythology and antiquities, written in collaboration with a colleague and published in six volumes between 1809 and 1825, the *Dizionario d'ogni mitologia e antichità, incominciato da Girolamo Pozzoli sulle tracce del Dizionario della favola di Fr. Noel, continuato ed ampliato dal Prof. Felice Romani e dal Dr. Antonio Peracchi*. What is to be remarked about this monumental work is that it deals with *all* mythologies and antiquities, and not only with those of the classical world.[1] There is, therefore, good reason to suppose that Romani's familiarity with the background of *Norma* would go rather beyond what any classical scholar would have picked up from reading in Tacitus about the remoter fringes of the Roman Empire, or browsing among the curious gleanings of the younger Pliny. He had been deeply involved in making available for Italian readers the best scholarship on ancient Celtic lore. It seems therefore appropriate to sharpen up our own imaginative perception of *Norma* by quoting from some of these articles.

'*Druidessa*' (the article is translated directly from Noël)
The wives of the druids shared in the esteem which the great mass of people had for their husbands, and like them took part in both political and religious affairs . . . above all they were celebrated for their skill in divination, and though at one time the druids had also taken part in prophecy, they had [latterly] abandoned this function to their wives almost entirely . . . there were other druidesses who lived celibate, and these were the Gauls' Vestals; and others again who, though married, lived regularly in the temples where they served . . . A third category was allotted to serve at the altars. The principal

office of the druidesses was to consult the stars, to take horoscopes and to predict the future, most often by consulting the entrails of the human victims they themselves sacrificed. Strabo has left us details of these atrocious ceremonies as they were practised among the Cimbri, who were a branch of the ancient Celts. On such occasions, he says, the druidesses were dressed in white; they went barefoot, and had a waistband woven of twigs. When the Cimbri had taken prisoners, those women ran up with swords in their hands, thrust the prisoners to the ground, and dragged them to the brink of a cistern, beside which was a kind of pavement on which stood the officiating druidess. One by one, as these unfortunates were led in front of her, she plunged a dagger into their breasts, and stood watching to see in what fashion the blood gushed out . . . Druidesses of the third category held nocturnal assemblies on the banks of swamps and marshes: there they consulted the moon, and performed a large number of superstitious ceremonies which attracted the scorn of the people.

Druidesses were even more respected among the Germans than among the Gauls. The former undertook nothing of importance without having first consulted these prophetesses, whom they regarded as inspired; and even when they were certain of victory, they would never have dared go into battle if the druidesses were opposed to it.

'*Eubagi*' (Noël, with additions by Pozzoli, Romani and Peracchi)
Name of a category of priests or philosophers among the Celts or Gauls. They were, according to Ammianus Marcellus and other historians, a group of druids who spent their time in research and in the contemplation of the mysteries of nature.

In the opinion of the authors cited by Noël, among the Greeks the word *eubage* corresponded to seer or holy man.

'*Irmasul*' (Noël, with additions by Pozzoli, Romani and Peracchi)
Synonym of Irmensul or Irminsul.

It is not known if this god was the God of War, the Greeks' *Ares*, the Latins' *Mars*, or whether it was the famous Irmin [Hermann], whom the Romans called *Arminio*, the conqueror of Varus and the avenger of German liberty.

In that part of ancient Germany which was inhabited by the Westphalian Saxons, close to the River Dimmel, rose a large hill, on which was situated the temple of Irminsul, in a township called . . . Eresburg. This temple, doubtless remarkable neither for its architecture, nor for the statue of the god, placed on a column, was most remarkable for the veneration it inspired in the people, who enriched it immensely by their offerings . . . The abbot of *Erperg*, who lived in the thirteenth century . . . assures us that the ancient Saxons worshipped only trees and streams, and that their god, the *Irminsul*, was itself nothing but the trunk of a tree stripped of its branches.

'*Vischio*' (mistletoe) (Noël, revised and amplified by Pozzoli, Romani and Peracchi)
A parasitic plant which attaches itself to oaks, and which, among the druids, was regarded as sacred. One of the most solemn religious ceremonies for

those priests consisted of gathering mistletoe . . . when mistletoe is found growing on an oak tree it is gathered with great solemnity, especially on the sixth day of the moon (which for these tribes marks the beginning of the month or year) . . . Hailing the moon with a native word meaning 'healing all things', they prepare a ritual sacrifice and banquet beneath a tree and bring up two white bulls with horns newly encircled with ribbons. A priest clad in white vestments climbs the tree and harvests the mistletoe, which is caught in a white cloak. Finally they sacrifice the victims, praying that the god's gift may be propitious for those on whom it is bestowed.

'*Luna*' (Noël)
The greatest pagan divinity after the sun. *Caesar* grants the peoples of the North and the ancient Germans no other gods except Fire, Sun and Moon. The cult of this last extended beyond the German ocean, and reached Saxony, Great Britain and Gaul, where the Moon had an oracle served by druidesses on the island of Sain, off the . . . coast of Brittany.

Norma was not Romani's first operatic excursion into the world evoked in these articles. In May 1820 *La sacerdotessa d'Irminsul*, with libretto by Romani and music by Giovanni Pacini, had its successful premiere at the Teatro Nuovo in Trieste. The opera was several times revived, in different Italian cities, but never published, and there is no reason to assume that Bellini knew it. Nevertheless, the title does make one sit up; when *Norma* was revived in Rome in 1834, papal censorship insisted that it be renamed *La foresta d'Irminsul* (Rinaldi 1965, p. 126).

Resemblances between *Norma* and Pacini's opera, which is set in the period of Charlemagne, are not close. However, Pacini's female protagonist, Romilda, is, like Norma, the Priestess of Irminsul, and an amorous rivalry that crosses the frontiers of race and religion is one of the mainsprings of the intrigue; here the rivalry focuses not on two women, but two men, Clodomiro, the Saxon prince, and Ruggiero, the general of Charlemagne's army. From time to time one finds situations in which Romani explores the kinds of emotional dilemma that will haunt the characters of *Norma*, and does so in remarkably similar words. Romilda, like Adalgisa, wrestles with the conflicting claims of love and religious duty:

> Io t'amo e la colpevol fiamma invan
> Tentai spegnar del Nume
> All'ara. Un Dio più forte
> Mi ti dipinge in ogni oggetto al guardo;
> Ma fuggo in van e mi distruggo ed ardo.

[I love you, and at the altar of my god I have vainly tried to extinguish the guilty passion. A more powerful god depicts you in every object I see. I flee in vain; I waste away and I burn.]

When, in the Act I finale, she is discovered by her High Priest father to be guilty of earthly passion, a confrontation develops between them that in some details anticipates the Act II finale of *Norma*:

Sacerdote: Con qual cor tradisti, o perfida,
Nume, patria, onore e fè?
Coro: Come del ciel il fulmine
Non piombò sopra te?
Romilda: Di scusarmi io non pretendo.
Degna pena è morte a me.
Padre ascolta . . .
Sacerdote: Intesi assai.
T'allontana, orror mi fai.
Sei l'obbrobio, indegna figlia,
Della mia canuta età.

[*High Priest:* Faithless one, how could your heart betray god, country, honour and faith? *Chorus:* Why did heaven's thunderbolt not fall on you? *Romilda:* I do not attempt to excuse myself. Death is fitting punishment for me. Father, listen . . . *High Priest:* I have heard enough. Away; you fill me with horror. Unworthy daughter, you are the shame of my old age.]

And in the Act II finale Ruggiero invites Romilda, for this is an opera that ends happily,

Sotto un cielo più sereno
Meco vieni a respirar.

[Come and live with me under a clearer sky.]

These are, of course, mere details in *La sacerdotessa d'Irminsul*. But it appears that Pacini himself regarded *Norma* as a too evident reworking of his own opera and fell out with Romani over it (*The New Grove Dictionary of Opera*, s.v. 'Romani'). In any case, it is worth bringing Pacini's opera into our story because it, and *Norma* too, are both examples of a theme that enjoyed a considerable vogue between the 1780s and the 1820s.

In the last quarter of the eighteenth century the literature of northern Europe tended increasingly to assert its differentness, its remoteness from that of the classical and Christian Mediterranean world. It was a tendency that combined the search for new aesthetic experiences (the vogue for Ossian) with nationalist or political aspirations (as in Klopstock's Hermann trilogy). Both Ossian (nostalgically) and

Klopstock (in hortatory style) had mirrored the clash of irreconcilable civilizations. This was a theme that could be put to fine tendentious purpose when the Napoleonic age arrived, and a new imperial civilization spread across Europe, calling into question local values, perverting local loyalties, destroying local customs, as the Roman Empire had once done.[2]

In Italy too there emerged a repertory of literature *à clef*, some of which – notably Monti's 'Bardo della selva nera' and Pindemonte's drama *Arminio* – bears upon Romani's *Norma* text. In terms of dramatic action, the parallels between *Arminio* and *Norma* are not close. *Arminio* depicts the greatest of all German warriors of old, Hermann the Cheruscan, vanquisher of Varus at the battle of the Teutoburger Wald, succumbing to the temptation to set himself up as an imperial monarch. (So the Napoleonic application is palpable.) He and his wife Thusnelda, whose pure Germanic character has been corrupted by a period of exile in Rome (in this she anticipates both Chateaubriand's Velleda and Soumet/Romani's Norma), are the central characters, whose inner conflicts, whose better and worse selves, are played upon by benign and malevolent counsellors. In the process their idealistic young son Baldéro is destroyed, and they come close to destroying the happiness of their daughter Velante too.

But though their plots are quite distinct, *Arminio* and *Norma* evidently belong to the same family of literary themes and the same imaginative world. Like *Norma*, *Arminio* is set in northern Europe at the time of the greatest reach of the Roman Empire. And it depicts a small, ostensibly primitive, community trying to find some *modus vivendi* with the overwhelming might, cultural as much as political, of a cosmopolitan empire – defining and clinging tenaciously to its own identity through its sense of place (notably the forest), through its own idiosyncratic social and moral traditions (tribal freedom, the veneration of women), and through its own particular decorum in religious and cultural life (the chorus of bards which closes each act, hymning the Teutonic gods, inculcating virtue, transfiguring the nation's own history in panegyric and elegy, and prophesying a glorious future).

Alexandre Soumet's *Norma*

It was the French playwright Alexandre Soumet, who knitted together all the strands I have been describing. The result, the five-act verse tragedy *Norma*, has been described as 'a bizarre and muddled encyclopaedia of barbarism' (Scherillo 1892, p. 652: in fairness it should be noted that Scherillo applies his description equally to *Les martyrs*). But it caught a mood of the time, and its premiere in April 1831 was given to clamorous acclaim. Only a few months later, Romani began to adapt it for Bellini's new opera. The following is a synopsis of Soumet's tragedy:

Act One (=Romani Act I, i–vi) The stage represents the sacred forest of the druids: the oak of Irminsul occupies the middle of the stage, and at its foot is visible a druidical stone which serves as an altar.

Flavius is alarmed at Pollion's intention of abandoning Norma for the beautiful young priestess Adalgise: it is only because of Norma's good will that the Romans have been able to keep the peace in Gaul for the last seven years.

Orovèse, the druids and Gaulish soldiers enter, discussing the prospects for throwing off the Roman yoke; Norma dampens their fervour, warning them that, without the support of the gods, any insurrection would be fruitless; and she reminds them that she is the medium through whom the gods make their will known. When Norma and Clotilde are left alone, it becomes clear that love takes priority in her heart over religious duty. Evidently Pollion has promised to take her and their sons back to Rome with him when his tour of duty is ended.

Adalgise has been warned by Norma of the gravity and folly of abandoning her vocation, and does her utmost to resist Pollion's amorous entreaties. The final scene in this first act is drawn on extensively in Romani's matching *Scena e Duetto*, and Soumet's curtain line, 'Oui, je le jure; / Adieu: ce n'est qu'au ciel que je serai parjure' [Yes, I swear it; / Farewell: it is only to heaven that I shall be forsworn], provides the clinching couplet of the lovers' cabaletta: 'Al mio Dio sarò spergiura, / Ma fedel a te sarò.'

Act Two (=Romani Act I, vii–ix) The stage represents a grove of trees and scattered rocks; an altar surmounted by a statue.

Norma's sons Agénor and Clodomir, for obvious reasons mere bystanders in the opera, have a crucial role in the play. In II.ii Agénor recounts a horrible dream, which Romani was to adapt to serve as Pollione's Act I *cantabile* 'Meco all'altar di Venere':

> D'un grand Hymen dans Rome on célébrait la fête.
> . . . des fleurs sur la tête,
> Les vierges d'Italie, en invoquant son nom,
> Conduisaient deux époux au temple de Junon . . .
> Mais j'ai vu tout à coup, ô prodige terrible,
> La fête se changer en sacrifice horrible!

[A great wedding ceremony was being celebrated in Rome . . . the virgins of Italy, with flowers on their heads, were conducting the bridal pair to Juno's temple, calling upon her name . . . But suddenly, oh terrible spectacle, I saw the ceremony change into a horrible slaughter!]

The Norma/Adalgise scene that follows provides much of the material detail of the great Act I duet in the opera: Adalgise abases herself before

Norma, confesses that she has betrayed her vocation as a novice priestess, gives a long account of her meetings with her Roman admirer and quotes various of the remarks he has made, and her account is punctuated, as it will be in the opera, by Norma's aside 'Comme moi, comme moi' [like me, like me]; the druidess goes on to release Adalgise from her vows so that she can marry. When Pollion appears and is recognized, Norma dismisses Adalgise and confronts him alone. She tries every kind of argument, every prayer, every threat to persuade him to take her back to Rome and make her his wife. Failing, she execrates him and threatens a horrible revenge: an episode that will provide the substance for the stretto of the Act I finale: 'Vanne, sì, mi lascia, indegno'.

In the final two scenes Soumet's act runs on to anticipate the events of the third act (and the second of the opera). Norma resolves to expiate her crimes, destroying herself and her sons in a conflagration of the temple she has betrayed.

Act Three (=Romani Act II, i–iii) The stage represents Norma's bedroom; a Roman bed covered with bear-skins.

After Clotilde has seen the boys settled for the night, Norma enters, carrying a lamp and a dagger. This second scene, 'Ils dorment tous les deux' [They are both sleeping], is the source for the *scena* 'Dormono entrambi'. At its climax 'she advances towards the bed, raises her dagger against them, and throws it down with a terrible cry'. Norma's screams wake the boys and she embraces them passionately. But she is determined to die, and summons Adalgise. She, learning for the first time that Pollion has been Norma's lover and that she has borne him two sons, renounces her own claim on him and undertakes to persuade him to return to Norma. Soumet provides models for both the 'Deh! con te' and the 'Mira, o Norma' movements of their duet, but nothing really comparable with the cabaletta 'Si, fino all'ore estreme'.

Act Four (=Romani Act II, vi–ultima) The stage represents the sacred forest of the druids; the oak of Irminsul, laden with the arms of the Gauls; a druidical stone centre-stage.

In Soumet's opening scenes, Norma awaits news of Adalgise's mission to Pollion, hears the report of her failure, and consequently resolves, 'Oui, le sang va couler; tous les Romains . . . Vengeance!' [Yes, blood is going to flow; all the Romans . . . Vengeance!]. Orovèse and the other druids enter for a ceremony during which Adalgise is to be consecrated priestess. Norma promptly redirects their thoughts to war, and leads them in a great spectacular sequence with music, in which the Gauls invoke their gods and the spirits of their ancestors to aid them as they fall upon the Romans, exterminating them or driving them from their land. Much of the spirit of Romani's II.vii is found here, perhaps also some hints for the choral scenes in Act I, but diffused through a spacious and spectacular ceremony rather than focused into a single explosive moment.

Thereafter the play provides the opera's model for most of the rest of the act: the capture of Pollion, the demands for his death, his defiance, Norma's weakening resolve, her solitary interrogation of him, her threats to their children, to the Romans, to Adalgise. The Gauls return: a sacrificial victim must still be found, and after much bloodthirsty shouting from the druids and much inner wrestling, Norma comes to her final resolution:

Moi-même,
Moi l'épouse des dieux, sacrilège, anathème,
Moi qu'un perfide amant jura d'aimer toujours,
Moi qu'il abandonnait, quand je sauvais ses jours,
Moi qui cherche à mourir et sans qu'il en pâlisse;
Le rejoins malgré lui dans un même supplice.

[I myself, I, the bride of the gods, sacrilegious, accursed, I, whom a faithless lover swore to love for ever, I, whom he was abandoning even as I was saving his life, I, who seek to die, yet at this he does not even turn pale; in despite of him, I shall be reunited with him in shared agony.]

She goes on to confess to the Gauls that she has profaned the temple with false prophecies to protect the Romans, and she throws herself on the altar with the cry,

Dieux sanglans, dieux jaloux, qui ne pouvent m'absoudre,
Proclamez mon forfait par le bruit de la foudre!
Et vous, armes d'airain, qui tressaillez d'effroi,
Sur mon front criminel tombez, écrasez-moi!

[Bloody gods, jealous gods, who cannot absolve me, proclaim my crime with the noise of the thunderbolt! And you, weapons of bronze which quiver with dread [those weapons, that is, that are suspended from the oak trees surrounding the Irminsul], fall on my criminal brow, crush me!]

But what in the Italian opera will be the climactic tragic scene of purgation, of terror and pity, is in the French play merely the beginning, the first of a whole series of frissons of horror. Orovèse anathematizes Norma, and she and Pollion are about to be led off to the scaffold when it is reported that the Roman battalions are attacking.

Soumet's **Act Five** is largely ignored in Romani's libretto (though its stage-set of lake, caverns and stone bridge was used for the otherwise freely invented fourth and fifth scenes of the opera's second act). Norma goes mad; she stabs one of her sons to death, and leaps with the other into a rocky abyss beyond the lake; Pollion, surrendering himself after a brief interlude of freedom, is led away by an inexorably vengeful Orovèse.

In many ways Romani's *Norma* libretto seems little more than a translation of the play. He has simplified, focused and redistributed the material with his customary deftness; but in terms of plot, characterization and even atmosphere there is little in his libretto for which some kind of precedent or model cannot be found. Nevertheless, in a number of vital ways he has transformed the character of Soumet's play. By eliminating the final act, and with it the horror and the madness inherited from the Medea stories, he transforms the drama into a purely human tragedy; by making Norma Oroveso's daughter, he draws the characters together into a more intimate web of feeling; by means of the choral scenes he romanticizes the austere tale, bringing the interior landscapes of the mind into harmony with the exterior landscape of moonlight and forest.

3 *Synopsis and musical frame*

Characters

Pollione: Roman pro-consul in Gaul	tenor
Oroveso: Chief druid	bass
Norma: Druidess; Oroveso's daughter	soprano
Adalgisa: A young priestess in the temple of Irminsul	soprano
Clotilde: Norma's confidante	soprano
Flavio: A friend of Pollione	tenor
Two boys, the sons of Norma and Pollione	

Chorus of druids, bards, eubages, priestesses, Gaulish warriors, and soldiers

The scene is set in Gaul, in the sacred forest and the temple of Irminsul.

[In the following synopsis indented passages in small type are stage-directions translated directly from the printed libretto.]

Act I, Scene 1

Sinfonia

Before the rise of the curtain, a full-length overture is played.

> The sacred forest of the druids; centre-stage the oak of Irminsul, at the foot of which can be seen the druidical stone which serves as an altar. Hills in the distance, covered with woods. It is night: distant fires glint through the trees.

No. 1 Coro d'Introduzione e Cavatina (Oroveso)

> To the strains of a sacred march the Gaulish hosts file in; then the procession of druids; finally Oroveso with the chief priests.

'Ite sul colle, o Druidi': Oroveso posts the druids to watch for the rising of the moon, which they are to announce with three strokes on the gong; then Norma will harvest the sacred mistletoe.

'Dell'aura tua profetica': They call upon Irminsul to inspire Norma with the gift of prophecy, and to fill her soul with hatred of the Romans: once she has given the word, they will rise up in revolt and drive their conquerors from the forests.

> They all disperse into the forest; from time to time their voices can still be heard in the distance. Then Flavio and Pollione enter cautiously from one side, wrapped in their togas.

In the terminology of the period an *introduzione* is 'everything that is sung between the end of the overture [*sinfonia*] and the first recitative' (Stendhal). Usually a substantial part of it is taken up with instrumental and choral scene-painting, the latter commonly entrusted to male voices only, as it is here. A cavatina is the aria in which a character makes his first entrance. As Norma's father, Oroveso has an important individual role to play in the final scene of the opera; for the rest he serves as choragus of the druids and Gauls. His cavatina is therefore less a free-standing aria than a song that arises out of, and sinks back into, the choral singing.

No. 2 Recitativo e Cavatina (Pollione)

A more common type of cavatina appears in Pollione's first scene. After a brief instrumental prelude and the recitative, the aria itself falls into two principal movements, the *cantabile* (sometimes called the *Andante*, *Adagio*, etc. according to its (slow) tempo marking) and the cabaletta, the two of them being linked together by a transitional *tempo di mezzo*. The *cantabile*, lyrical in style, and the cabaletta, brilliant or at least energetic, embody the contrasting facets, retrospective and forward-looking, of the singer's mind. In the present case the *cantabile* is a narrative, longer and looser-limbed in structure than usual. The remainder of the scene is notable for the continual reminders of the lurking presence of the Gauls: the *tempo di mezzo* is in large part sustained by the distant sounds of their ceremonials, and the cabaletta is, as it were, infected by them, adopting their key, their tempo and much of their rhythmic and melodic character. As was customary, the cabaletta is sung twice.

Recitativo: Flavio reminds Pollione of Norma's warning – it is death for them to be found in this part of the forest. Norma's name freezes Pollione's blood: he confesses to his friend that he has fallen in love with the young priestess Adalgisa. A more than human power drives him on in a course of action that he recognizes to be suicidal; for Norma still loves him, and has borne him two children; her wrath will be appalling.

Cantabile, 'Meco all'altar di Venere': He recounts a terrifying dream – he and Adalgisa were marrying in the temple of Venus in Rome, amid the chanting of hymns and the wafting of incense. Suddenly a spectre wrapped in druidical robes appeared; a thunder-bolt fell on the altar; darkness descended and silence; Adalgisa vanished; groans and the wailing of children were heard; and a terrible voice from the depths of the temple cried, 'Thus Norma wreaks havoc on a traitor in love.'

Tempo di mezzo: The sound of the sacred gong announces the rising of the moon.

Cabaletta, 'Mi protegge, mi difende': The love that inspires Pollione is a greater power than the Irminsul served by these barbarians; if necessary he will, to win Adalgisa, burn down their forests and smash the altars of their god.

No. 3 Coro – Scena e Cavatina (Norma)

(a) Coro

The druids return, together with the priestesses, warriors, bards, eubages, sacrificers, and with Oroveso in their midst.

'Norma viene: le cinge la chioma': Norma is approaching, robed for the mistletoe ceremony. The Gauls foresee the waning of Rome's star, while Irminsul roams through the night sky like a comet of ill omen. The chorus is, in effect, the first movement of the ceremony, the prelude to the great *Scena e Cavatina* that introduces Norma herself.

(b) Scena e Cavatina (Norma)

Norma in the midst of her priestesses. Her hair is loose, her brow ringed with a crown of vervain, and in her hand she carries a golden sickle. She takes up a position on the druidical stone, and gazes around like one inspired. All fall silent.

Scena, 'Sediziose voci': Norma reproves those who dare to raise the voice of rebellion in this sacred place. But the druids are impatient: how much longer must the Roman eagle be allowed to contaminate their forests and temples? Let the sword of Brennus be unsheathed once more.[1] It will be unsheathed in vain, retorts Norma, if they attack prematurely; the enemy is still too strong. She has read in the book of Fate that Rome will fall, not by the hand of its enemies, but consumed by its own vices.

She cuts the mistletoe with her sickle; the priestesses gather it in baskets woven from osiers. Norma advances, raising her arms to the heavens. The moon shines in full splendour. All prostrate themselves.

Cantabile, 'Casta Diva': Norma leads the prayer to the chaste moon goddess – may she calm their too ardent hearts, spreading the same peace on earth as she spreads through the heavens.

Tempo di mezzo: The ceremony finished, she commands all those who are not ministers of Irminsul to leave the sacred forest. When the god requires their service in slaughtering the Romans, she will summon them again. They assure her they will be ready; and no-one will they kill with greater relish than the hated pro-consul Pollione. Norma agrees.

Cabaletta, 'Ah! bello a me ritorna': But in her heart she knows that as long as he is faithful to her (for she begins to fear his passion is cooling), she will defend Pollione against the world.

Norma departs, and all follow her in due order.

A *scena* distinguishes itself from a recitative by the greater range of its musical resources: here the chorus is involved as well as the soloists, and the *scena* closes in prophetic vein, in part sustained by regular orchestral figurations, in part (the last five bars) rising to the eloquence of arioso. The *cantabile* 'Casta Diva', a liturgical aria, as it were, rather than an outpouring of personal feeling, is more formal than the matching movement in Pollione's cavatina. In fact it is strophic, with a long instrumental introduction, and a solo/choral interlude between the two strophes. And while Pollione's cabaletta was energetic and emphatic, Norma's is florid in style. But in this scene too the druid music is ever-present, setting the tone for the *tempo di mezzo*, and recurring again to play the Gauls out after Norma's cabaletta is finished. The effect of these regular recurrences of the solemnly or vigorously marching themes of the Gauls is to bind together the whole sequence of opening scenes into the kind of massive musico-dramatic tableau that Bellini must have admired in Rossini and Spontini.

No. 4 Scena e Duetto (Adalgisa, Pollione)

The first part of the act closes with the first of the opera's great duets. In principle a duet is based on the same dichotomy of lyrical reflection (*cantabile*) and energetic anticipation (cabaletta) as a solo scene. Commonly, however, these core elements are preceded by an additional first movement (*primo tempo* or *tempo d'attacco*) in which the characters meet, or find, or confront one another. Such a *tempo d'attacco* is usually freer in form and more declamatory in style than the *cantabile* or cabaletta: often it employs a '*parlante*' technique in which the musical continuity is provided by the reiteration, variation and development of an orchestral theme. In the present case the functions of *tempo d'attacco*, *cantabile* and *tempo di mezzo* are combined in the first movement of the duet.

Scena, 'Sgombra è la sacra selva': Adalgisa enters, wrestling with the dilemma that torments her – she has fallen in love with a Roman and, for all her religious vows, cannot get him out of her thoughts. She throws herself on the altar praying for Irminsul's protection. Pollione and Flavio approach. Dismissing his friend's warning, Pollione urges Adalgisa to abandon the worship of a god who causes her such distress; Love is a more fitting divinity for her to serve.

Tempo d'attacco/Cantabile/Tempo di mezzo, 'Va, crudele, al Dio spietato': If she insists on keeping faith with this savage god, he goes on, she will be able to offer up Pollione's blood as a sacrifice, for nothing will persuade him to renounce her. Adalgisa retorts that the cost to her is no less bitter: she is perjured and tormented by guilt, and the heavens have hidden themselves in dark clouds. Let her then come to Rome, argues Pollione, where the skies are brighter and the gods more generous.

Cabaletta, 'Vieni in Roma, ah! vieni, o cara': While Pollione paints a beguiling picture of a future life together, Adalgisa makes one last effort to break free; finally, however, she yields to Pollione's entreaties, vowing to elope with him on the morrow.

Act I, Scene 2[2]

Norma's dwelling place.

No. 5 Finale

(a) Scena e Duetto (Norma, Adalgisa)

The change of scene is underlined by a tonal dislocation more abrupt than anything we have hitherto heard (A♭–A minor) and a prelude more extensive. There is no *tempo d'attacco* in the duet. Instead the *cantabile* steals up on Norma and Adalgisa as they converse, so that the closing phrases of their recitative are superimposed upon the instrumental introduction to 'Sola, furtiva al tempio'.

Scena, 'Vanne, e li cela entrambi': Norma cannot look at her sons without being troubled by a strange conflict of emotions – love and hatred, joy and sorrow. For Pollione has been recalled to Rome, and she does not yet know whether he intends to take them with him. As Adalgisa is heard approaching, Norma embraces the boys and Clotilde leads them away.

Adalgisa has asked to speak with Norma in confidence. She confesses that she has fallen in love; that all her efforts to overcome her feelings have failed, and that now she has sworn to abandon altar and home to follow the man she loves. Sympathetically Norma invites her to tell her exactly what has happened, and Adalgisa begins her story: one day, as she was praying at the altar a man came into the temple; she fell in love with him.

Cantabile, 'Sola, furtiva al tempio': She goes on to admit that, since then, they have met regularly, their passion growing day by day; she remembers every word he says to her, and all her everyday experiences are transfigured by her love. As Adalgisa tells her tale, Norma muses, reflecting how exactly the girl's experiences and emotions resemble her own when she first fell in love. She reassures her young charge: the oath she has taken as a priestess is not yet an eternally binding one.

Cabaletta, 'Ah sì, fa core, abbracciami': Not only does Norma forgive the overjoyed Adalgisa; she releases her from her vows and wishes her all happiness.

(b) Scena e Terzetto (Norma, Adalgisa, Pollione)

What was said above about the form of the duet applies *mutatis mutandis* to a larger-scale ensemble too, even when, as here, it serves as finale to an act. A number of special factors do, however, apply: the *scena* is likely to contain a richer variety of material; the quick closing movement is called a stretta rather than a cabaletta; and, most important, the *cantabile* of the Act I finale (of the Act II finale in a three- or four-act opera) will be motivated by the most thrilling peripeteia in the whole drama. For that reason it is often composed in such a way as to heighten the effect of 'freeze'.

Scena, 'Ma dì'; l'amato giovane': Norma is disconcerted to learn that the object of Adalgisa's affections is not a Gaul but a Roman. When

Pollione appears and, to his own discomfiture, is acknowledged by Adalgisa, Norma's anger knows no bounds and she pours out her contempt for the Roman.

> [Adalgisa] covers her face with her hands. Norma grasps her by the arm and forces her to look at Pollione.

Andante, 'Oh! di qual sei tu vittima': Norma solemnly warns Adalgisa that she is the victim of a treacherous seducer; it were better to have died than to have fallen into the hands of such a man; he will betray Adalgisa as he has betrayed Norma herself. While Adalgisa can express only astonishment and consternation, Pollione demands that Norma spare him her reproaches, and spare Adalgisa the shameful details of their past.

Tempo di mezzo: It is his destiny to love Adalgisa and to abandon Norma. The druidess challenges him to follow that destiny and Adalgisa to follow him. But Adalgisa, now she realizes what kind of man Pollione is, would rather die.

Stretta, 'Vanne, sì, mi lascia, indegno': Norma's anger flares up again. Woe betide Pollione if he abandons her and the children, imagining that he will ever enjoy another woman's love: the furies of her vengeance will haunt him everywhere. The Roman, as roused as Norma herself, retorts that he is in the grip of a passion far greater than anything she can threaten.

The temple gongs sound, summoning Norma to the sacred rites. She and Adalgisa warn Pollione that they ring a death-knell for him. He is unmoved; ready, if need be, to face death, but determined first to destroy their barbarous god. He rushes away.

Act II, Scene 1

> Inside Norma's dwelling place. On one side a Roman bed covered with bear-skins. Norma's sons are sleeping. Norma with a lamp and a dagger in her hand. She sits and places the lamp on the table. She is pale, changed out of all recognition.

No. 6 Scena e Duetto

(a) Scena (Norma)

An extensive instrumental prelude precedes the *scena*. The same material provides the principal feature of both parts: a grand cello cantilena, which recurs in the *scena* as the arioso, 'Teneri, teneri figli'.

Scena, 'Dormono entrambi': Norma is relieved to find her sons asleep, for she has resolved to kill them, and would not have them see the hand that does the deed. They cannot live: for they will be killed if they stay in Gaul, and if they go to Rome and the care of a stepmother they will suffer a shame worse than death. But now she freezes in her tracks, appalled at the thought of destroying her loved ones. What have they done that is wrong? The answer is clear: they are the sons of Pollione; and since they are already dead for her, let them die for him too.

> She advances towards the bed and raises her dagger; she gives a horrified scream; the boys wake up . . . she embraces them and weeps.

She calls Clotilde and asks her to summon Adalgisa.

(b) Scena e Duetto (Norma, Adalgisa)

This number includes all the customary features of a full-scale duet, each of them in its appointed place. Noteworthy is the fact that each successive movement contains a smaller proportion of solo singing, so that the cabaletta – and this is clearly a reflection of its expressive purpose – is sung *a due* throughout.

Scena, 'Mi chiami, o Norma?': No longer ashamed to have the depths of her degradation revealed to Adalgisa, Norma exacts from her a promise, which the girl readily gives. Resolved on suicide, Norma wishes to entrust her sons to Adalgisa, who is to take them to the Roman camp. If Pollione and she are properly married perhaps he will be less cruel to her than he has been to Norma. Adalgisa is appalled.

Tempo d'attacco, 'Deh! con te, con te li prendi': Norma persists – Adalgisa should care for the boys and protect them; she asks no privileges for them, only that they should not be abandoned or enslaved. Adalgisa declines the charge: when she promised to fulfil Norma's request she imagined herself doing something good, not assenting to her death. Rather than that, she will employ all her powers of eloquence to win back Pollione's love for Norma.

Andante, 'Mira, o Norma, a' tuoi ginocchi': While Adalgisa urges Norma to abandon her dreadful scheme out of pity for her sons, Norma is reluctantly beguiled by hopes which she knows to be illusory.

Tempo di mezzo: Gradually Adalgisa wins Norma over. Certainly she did love Pollione; but now Norma's friendship is more important to her. If she cannot restore her happiness, the pair of them must hide themselves from mankind for ever.

Cabaletta, 'Sì, fino all'ore estreme': They swear eternal friendship; somewhere the earth will have a hiding place for them, and as long as they are true to one another they can face whatever fate has in store.

Act II, Scene 2

A lonely place close to the druids' forest, surrounded by ravines and caves. In the background a lake crossed by a stone bridge. Gaulish warriors.

No. 7 Coro e Sortita (Oroveso)

For a character who has already sung a cavatina to return to sing a *sortita* is most curious; for a *sortita*, like a cavatina, is an entrance aria. Probably this terminological tautology is a relic of the changes of structure undergone by the opera as Bellini worked on it (see Chapter 4). In this aria too, a single-movement *cantabile*, Oroveso's identity is scarcely to be differentiated from that of the rest of the druids and Gauls who sing with him.

Coro, 'Non partì?': The noises from the Roman camp show that Pollione has not yet left. The Gauls await his departure eagerly.

Sortita, 'Guerrieri, a voi venirne' – 'Ah! del Tebro al giogo indegno': Oroveso enters. Hopes that the revolt was soon to begin are disappointed, for Pollione's appointed successor is an even more feared and cruel warrior. The Gauls cannot understand why Norma does not therefore command them to strike now, before the new pro-consul arrives. Oroveso urges patience and submission to the will of the gods. He shares their hatred of the Roman yoke; but the more they keep their true feelings hidden, the more devastating will be the effect when at last they take up arms.

1. 'Luogo solitario', Act II, Scene 2; Alessandro Sanquirico's design for the Milan premiere of *Norma*.

Act II, Scene 3

The temple of Irminsul. An altar to one side.

No. 8 Finale

(a) Scena e Coro

Scena, 'Ei tornerà': Norma fondly imagines a suppliant Pollione returning to her arms; but when Clotilde reports that Adalgisa's mission has failed, her jealousy flares up, and she suspects her young colleague of plotting an escape from her tutelage. Clotilde points out that Adalgisa *has* come back, very sad, but eager to resume her vows, while Pollione is threatening to carry her off from the very altar itself. Norma resolves to avert so intolerable an affront by launching the revolt. She hurries to the altar and strikes thrice on the shield that hangs there. Oroveso, druids, bards, priestesses stream into the temple, and Norma takes up her position on the altar. The time is ripe, she tells them, for war.

Coro, 'Guerra, guerra! le galliche selve': The Gauls break into their war-hymn – War, war! the forests are as full of warriors as of trees, and they will fall upon the Romans like starving wolves on the flocks. Blood, blood! their axes will be steeped in blood, and blood will gurgle mournfully down the waters of the Loire. Slaughter, extermination, revenge! the Roman armies will fall like corn before the scythe; the Roman eagle will be hurled to the ground.

(b) Scena e Duetto (Norma, Pollione)

The number is a long and continuous conversation; and once the duet proper begins, at 'In mia man', Romani writes the whole scene in rhyming *ottonario* metre. It would be misleading to say that Bellini composes it *in* the traditional *cantabile / tempo di mezzo /* cabaletta form; rather, passages that are *cantabile*-like, transitional, and cabaletta-like emerge with the minimum of formality from this continuing conversation. Although it is called a duet, there is no two-part singing whatsoever until the *più vivo* cadences at the close of the 'cabaletta'.

Scena, 'Né compi il rito, o Norma?': As Oroveso asks who is to be the required sacrificial victim, a tumult is heard off-stage. Clotilde reports that a Roman has been captured trespassing in the precinct of the novice priestesses. Pollione is led in, and the Gauls recognize that their victim has been found. He refuses to answer Oroveso's questions, and Norma takes up the sacred sword to kill him. But she finds herself overwhelmed by her emotions, and on the pretext of needing to interrogate him, demands to be left alone with him.

Cantabile, 'In mia man alfin tu sei': Norma tells Pollione that she alone has the power to save him, and is willing to do so on one condition – that he take a solemn oath to go away and make no attempt to see Adalgisa again. Pollione refuses; he would rather die than be guilty of such cowardice. Norma continues: they have two children; once already she has been close to killing them, and it would take very little more to make her forget she is a mother.

Tempo di mezzo, 'Ah! crudele, in sen del padre': As for killing Pollione, does he imagine that one Roman is sufficient sacrifice? They will be slaughtered in their hundreds; and there is Adalgisa too, who, for betraying her vows, should be burned to death.

Cabaletta, 'Già mi pasco ne' tuoi sguardi': By now, Norma is swept away on a mood of terrible exultation to see Pollione grovelling as wretchedly as she has had to do, as despairing as she has been.

2. 'Tempio di Irminsul', Act II, Scene 3; Alessandro Sanquirico's design for the Milan premiere of *Norma*.

(c) Scena ed Aria Finale (Norma)

The finale is more accurately perceived as a *concertato* led by Norma than as a solo aria. Each of its movements is really a *cantabile*, and in fact it is the first, if only by virtue of its symmetries and repetitions, that more resembles a (slow) cabaletta/stretta than the second.

Scena, 'Dammi quel ferro': Norma calls back the Gauls. She has another victim for their sacrifice, she tells them: a priestess who has broken her vows and betrayed her country; let the funeral pyre be prepared for her too. But as she is about to name Adalgisa, conscience gets the better of her. How can she charge an innocent girl with crimes of which she is guilty herself? To the horror and incredulity of her people, she names herself as the sacrificial victim.

Largo [concertato 1], 'Qual cor tradisti': The Roman has failed in his attempt to abandon Norma; they will be united in death as in life, united on the sacrificial pyre, united in the tomb. Pollione at last perceives the nobility of the woman he has so casually betrayed. Oroveso and the Gauls still cling to the hope that there may be some escape from this horror: perhaps Norma has lost her reason; the god himself has given no sign of anger.

Tempo di mezzo: When they call upon Norma to exculpate herself, she insists that she is guilty beyond their imagining. For in the meantime, she and Pollione have remembered their sons. She confesses to Oroveso that she is a mother and beseeches him to care for the boys. The old priest, heart-broken and appalled, refuses and dismisses Norma from his presence.

Più moderato [concertato 2], 'Deh! non volerli vittime': Norma intensifies her prayer – let the children not suffer because of her sins; let Oroveso have compassion on their innocence, for they are his own flesh and blood. Her father's love overcomes his rigour; he weeps tears of pity and forgiveness, and Norma and Pollione can face death with equanimity. She is stripped of her accoutrements of sanctity and covered in a black veil. The Gauls anathematize her, and she bids farewell to her weeping father, while Pollione [Norma too in the libretto, but not in Bellini's setting] sees their shared death as the beginning of a more holy love that will last for eternity.

4 *Music and poetry*

In the eyes of contemporary critics Bellini was a 'philosophical' composer; that is to say, a composer whose music, unlike that of his great predecessor Rossini, was intimately linked with the poetry he set. Sometimes this perception led to his being described as 'the restorer of true Italian music', faithful to the precepts of the classical training of the Naples conservatories[1] – to those, for example, of one of his own teachers, Girolamo Crescentini, who declared, for all the world like some Renaissance humanist, that 'il canto deve essere un'imitazione del discorso' (song must be an imitation of speech) (Maguire 1989, p. 45). Bellini's relationship with his librettist Felice Romani was therefore the most critical artistic relationship of his career, more important to the unfolding and development of his genius even than his associations with Pasta or with Rubini. 'If Romani had not been,' remarked Francesco Regli, 'Italy would have had no Bellini' (quoted in Rinaldi 1965, p. 351).

When Bellini first met Romani, shortly after his arrival in Milan in the spring of 1827, he had been a practising librettist for some thirteen years, producing anything up to half a dozen librettos in a typical season, most of them for La Scala. He was a vastly more experienced man of the theatre than Bellini himself, and had worked with all the important Italian composers of the age. But from the first, Bellini exerted a special fascination over him, and prompted a greater measure of solicitude than any of the others with whom Romani had worked. In a tribute written after Bellini's untimely death in 1835, the poet recalled his first impressions: he had divined, he claimed, 'a passionate heart, a mind ambitious to soar beyond the sphere in which it was restrained by academic rules and the servility of imitation. [From the first] . . . we understood one another, and we struggled united against the vicious conventions of the musical theatre, girding ourselves to eradicate them little by little, by dint of courage, perseverance and love' (quoted in Rinaldi 1965, p. 195).

Doubtless there is an element of misty-eyed nostalgia in these recollections, and sceptical critics have insisted that there is not in principle a distinction to be made between the librettos Romani wrote for Bellini and those he wrote for other composers (see, for example, Lippmann, in Adamo and Lippmann 1981, pp. 358–9). But there is no doubt that he was prepared to go to enormous trouble to try to satisfy the demands Bellini made on him, and the composer's reliance rapidly became an obsessional dependence. From *Il pirata* onwards, every one of the eight operas composed by Bellini before he left Italy for France and England in 1833 had a libretto by Romani.[2] In its exclusiveness, its productiveness and its clear aesthetic purpose, it is one of the three or four most remarkable composer–librettist relationships in the history of opera.

Any attempt to analyse Bellini's music in isolation from Romani's poetry will therefore be sterile; and in this chapter I examine poetry and music together, commenting on the formal layout of the libretto and its points of particular dramatic and psychological interest, before addressing the way in which Bellini has drawn out, amplified or transformed its character.

Norma is a 'number-opera', an opera of arias, duets, choruses and finales. But it is also a 'scene-opera', in which the individual solos and ensembles and choruses that fall within a particular 'scene' (using the word in the sense of a piece of continuous dramatic action taking place at a single time, in a single setting) are linked together by musical continuity, by tonal coherence, and, sometimes, by thematic recurrences. A simple example would be the first scene of Act II, the Prelude, *Scena* and *Scena e Duetto* set in Norma's dwelling. The musical flow is unbroken; it unfolds in a simple tonal progression from the D minor of the prelude, via C major to the F major in which the duet closes; the principal thematic material of the first *scena* is drawn from that of the prelude. A more ambitious example of the same kind of musical thinking is the opening scene of Act I, built round the mistletoe ceremony, and comprising the *Coro d'Introduzione e Cavatina* for Oroveso, the *Recitativo e Cavatina* of Pollione, a chorus and the *Scena e Cavatina* of Norma. Stylistically and thematically this complex is unified by the recurrence of the marches and march-like music associated with the Gauls, and (if 'Casta Diva' is sung in its original G major key) it is contained within a tonal orbit of G, C, E♭ and G again; until, in Norma's cabaletta, she escapes into the world of her own private emotions with a shift to F major.

The basis of this number/scene structure is, of course, to be found in the libretto, which, in common with all Italian librettos down virtually to the end of the nineteenth century, makes a clear distinction between verses written for recitative or *scene* – a free alternation of *settenari* and *endecasillabi* with occasional rhyme (they are commonly called *versi sciolti*, though it is more strictly correct to describe them as *versi a selva* and restrict the use of the term *versi sciolti* to blank verse) – and verses written for arias and ensembles, which are organized in strophic patterns, regular in both metre and rhyme.

The range of Romani's metres in *Norma* is surprisingly narrow. In two choruses, 'Norma viene' in I.iii and 'Guerra, guerra!' in II.vii, he employs the anapaestic *decasillabi* that Manzoni had made fashionable; the final scene makes extensive use of *quinari accoppiati*; sometimes, for example in II.i for 'Dormono entrambi' and at the start of the final scene, 'All'ira vostra', the *versi a selva* of the recitative are amplified into genuine *versi sciolti*. Apart from this, the final definitive form of the libretto makes exclusive use of *versi a selva* for the recitatives, and of *settenari* and *ottonari* for the lyrical movements; the vast paragraphs of *ottonario* verse are in fact without precedent in Italian opera (Mariano 1990, p. 196). The one aria that Romani did write in *quinari* was sent back by Bellini for rewriting, and another aria in *decasillabi*, 'Tutti, ah, tutti tradisco i suoi voti' was apparently rejected by the censor (Branca 1882, p. 169).

Though the formal principles on which the *Norma* libretto is designed are, for the most part, the commonplaces of the Italian repertory in the years around 1830, its artistic qualities are unique. Romani himself took a particular pride in the opera, describing it, in relation to the rest of the Bellini canon, as 'la più bella rosa della ghirlanda' (*Gazzetta piemontese*, 8 April 1836, quoted in Rinaldi 1965, p. 277). Among Bellini's near-contemporaries, both Wagner and Schopenhauer acclaimed it with unqualified enthusiasm as a very model of what a tragic opera libretto ought to be (see Chapter 7). For a time it even acquired, like the *drammi* of Metastasio a century earlier, the status of a work of literature in its own right; in 1864 Carlo d'Ormeville concocted a spoken *Norma* for Adelaide Ristori, 'calmly mixing together the texts of Soumet and Romani' (Tintori 1983, p. 181). There is nothing conventionally romantic about the tragic love-triangle in *Norma* – there is no tyrant, no Byronic exile or outsider. Instead, within a plot of rare dignity and simplicity are focused all the finest aspirations of the best operatic minds of the age: to restore or recreate the tragic art of ancient Greece; to bring to opera a more true and life-like psychology; to postulate a timely new ideal of nationhood, by showing protagonists and people bound together in a free and spiritual unity of purpose. One is surely very close to the aspirational ideal Romani himself defined for men of letters: 'to describe the customs, treat the passions, scourge the vices and exalt the virtues of the nation' (Quoted in Rinaldi 1965, p. 193).

Clearly space does not permit a full account of the entire opera. I have therefore focused my discussion on the opening scenes, set in the sacred forest of the druids, and the Act II finale.

Act I (Scene 1)

No. 1 Coro d'Introduzione e Cavatina (Oroveso)

A setting of I.i of Romani's libretto.

In my synopsis I quoted the stage-directions in full because, throughout the opera, the picturesque and evocative values of the setting are of primary importance. Nowhere is this more true than in this *Introduzione*. It is night,[3] there are forests near and far; fires gleam through the trees; the sacred and terrible oak of Irminsul and the druidic altar dominate the scene. Even the stage-action, essentially a religious procession and recession, is little more than an adjunct to this stage-picture.

Oroveso begins his address with due emphasis on the sacred, but the thrust of the scene gradually shifts towards the kind of political agitation which both Caesar and Tacitus noted as characteristic of the druids (Piggott 1968, pp. 97–8, 109). The druidic rank and file vociferate menacingly; peace is ignominious; Irminsul is a 'terribil Dio', invoked to inspire hatred and wrath. Much emphasis is laid on the eagle that symbolizes Roman power, a subversive stroke, in Branca's view, for the Habsburg dynasty likewise symbolized its 'caesarian' authority with an imperial eagle; it was, for example, the 'logo' of the official *Gazzetta privilegiata di Milano* (Branca 1882, p. 172; Rinaldi 1965, p. 88).[4]

Romani's continuous *settenari*, laid out in three eight-line stanzas, make no formal distinction between the scene-setting for the moonlit rites and the outburst of hatred against the Romans. But they do have something of the dynamic of the *cantabile/tempo di mezzo*/cabaletta type of scene. The first stanza is for Oroveso alone ('Ite sul colle, o Druidi'), the second is dominated by the druids, the third is another solo for Oroveso ('Sì: parlerà terribile'). Bellini models his musical structure less on that poetic structure, however, than on the dramatic sense: he breaks off Oroveso's *cantabile* prematurely, turning the last two lines of the eight-line stanza ('Tre volte annunzi il mistico / Bronzo sacerdotal') into part of a *tempo di mezzo* which, by means of rapping military rhythms and a series of unstable modulatory harmonies, propels the music with a new sense of gathering storm; and he starts the 'cabaletta' with the druids, in the middle of Romani's second verse, thereby making the point that it is the priestly/popular voice that takes the lead in demanding the expulsion of the Romans from Gaul. The typical cabaletta repetitiveness is achieved not so much *within* Oroveso's solo as between the chorus and the soloist.

But there is another architectural pressure to which Bellini responds in this scene; for by enclosing it in unusually integral and vivid stage-directions for a processional and recessional 'marcia religiosa', Romani gives the cue for a tableau that is in an overall ternary form. The orchestral prelude evolves into a solemn march which accompanies the druids' entrance and, in due course, their exit. Moreover, as Oroveso's first address directs the druids on their way ('Ite sul colle'), the preludial material is heard again during that – indeed his '*cantabile*' is really an arioso superimposed upon a restatement of the prelude, suitably compressed and modified.

Within this overall structure there is a great deal of finer rhetorical or dramatic detail.

The darkness and stillness of the scene are mirrored in the low-pitched prelude and its pedal points. The opening bars are a notable essay in nocturnal scoring, with an important role for the bassoons, with divided violas and cellos moving above a double-bass foundation, and occasional telling contributions from timpani, soft horns and trombones.

The appearance of the druids is marked by the entry of the stage-band, the *banda*, a quasi-Verdian piece of instrumental rhetoric which yet lacks the directness of such effects in Verdi since the band does not actually play the march, it merely marks the harmonies. On the other hand the unison choral writing at 'Dell'aura tua profetica', prompting rather than led by Oroveso's aria, is clearly a source of

Verdi's 'risorgimental' manner. The dotted rhythms and what Friedrich Lippmann likes to describe as the 'isorhythmic' organization of the phrases make this a good example of the emphatic plainness that became so popular during the 1830s. At the same time, the triplet broken chord patterns in the inner strings, which Bellini layers up at three different pitches – for cellos, violas, second violins – give the music a pulsing inner excitement. When the opening music recurs for the recessional, an undercurrent of unrest remains, embodied in triplets, cross-rhythms (cf. the marking '*spasmodico*' three bars before Fig. 18), sinister flecks of chromatic colour. A realistic fading away of voices into the distance closes the number.

The scene provides as good an illustration of Bellini's harmonic resource as any in the opera. The tonic key of G major is rarely departed from except for a series of dramatically or rhetorically motivated 'feints'. The prelude heightens expectancy for the arrival of the druids with a long pedal on the dominant of the dominant, and it heightens expectancy for the start of the arioso/*cantabile* with energetic chromaticism and a dominant pedal. In the *tempo di mezzo* too the purpose of the modulation – essentially a mediant pedal that Bellini simply drops on to – is to create a sense of tension that can be discharged with the start of the 'cabaletta'. The mediant modulations within the cabaletta serve primarily to highlight the returns of the principal theme.

Clearly this number is no mere introduction. It is a prime example of the new status that the chorus was beginning to enjoy in Italian romantic opera, encouraged by Manzoni's poetic dramas, and very likely in part inspired by Madame de Staël's profoundly influential *De l'Allemagne*, with its reflections on the use of the chorus in Schiller's *Die Braut von Messina* and in other German dramatists (see Engelhardt 1988, p. 21). Altogether it is one of the most 'romantic' episodes in the whole of Bellini's *oeuvre*. I use the term 'romantic', partly because, in Franca Cella's words, 'in the romantic age the sense of place signifies the life of the people' (Cella 1968, p. 519), usually a people who were exemplary for their audiences in their love of their native land and the fervour with which they longed for its liberty; but even more in tribute to the care with which Bellini evokes a remote and mysterious setting, the *nemeton* or holy place deep in the northern forest (see Piggott 1968, p. 80). Even critics who tended to be a little condescending have admired his evocation of atmosphere here:

'but Bellini was picturesque', concedes Chorley. 'In spite of the inexperience with which the instrumental score is filled up, the opening scene of "Norma", in the dim druidical wood, bears the true character of antique sylvan mystery' (Chorley 1862, vol. I, p. 101). 'As in Leopardi', remarks Cella, 'the messianic suspense is transformed into landscape' (Cella 1968, p. 519).

No. 2 Recitativo e Cavatina (Pollione)

A setting of I.ii of Romani's libretto.

After the London premiere of *Norma* in June 1833, a reporter for *Galignani's Messenger* wrote, 'The opera had no arias.' The observation seems both bizarre and fatuous; but it serves to highlight how far Bellini's more old-fashioned contemporaries felt he was going in breaking with traditional formal categories. How Oroveso was, so to speak, sucked up by the chorus we have already seen; how the prima donna's expected final aria was dissolved into a grand finale, we shall see in due course. Adalgisa has no aria at all. In the meantime, however, both leading characters do sing cavatinas; *Galignani's Messenger* prompts us to note that both are unusual.

Pollione's cavatina introduces us to an unusual kind of protagonist: neither a hero nor a plain villain, but a man in whose heart is focused the conflict of northern and southern worlds on which the drama turns. For men from the Mediterranean the great forests of northern Europe were haunted by many a nameless terror. For much of this scene Pollione is a frightened man, creeping furtively about, wrapped in his toga, chilled by his dread of Norma, driven by a passion which appals him and which he knows will destroy him, haunted by guilt. That he is the plaything of Fate becomes clear when his first musical number proves to be the recounting of a dream; for to begin an opera with a dream is to single out the dreamer as the chosen victim of Fate. Branca reports that at an early age Romani had a heightened susceptibility to phantasms and the paranormal, and he retained an almost morbid interest in dreams and prophecies ('Meco all'altar' is both), and anything that could be perceived as a supernatural intervention into human affairs (Branca 1882, p. 262, quoted by Lippmann, in Adamo and Lippmann 1981, p. 340). Strophe one of the aria describes the world to which Pollione longs to escape: Rome – the temple of Love, Adalgisa dressed as a bride, flowers, music, incense, exquisite delights. All this is blocked out in strophe two by phenomena from the world in which he is now obliged to live: dark shadows, druidic robes, thunderbolt, eclipse, silence. Strophe three takes the form of a prophetic warning, fuelled by his conscience: Adalgisa will vanish, your children will weep; for Norma will be revenged on a traitor in love.

The *cantabile* 'Meco all'altar' is a narrative aria of three eight-line stanzas, still, like the whole of Scene 1, in *settenari*. The *tempo di mezzo* continues in the same metrical style, likewise forming an eight-line paragraph, but now in dialogue form and with a less highly wrought rhyme-scheme. The cabaletta is supplied by a single eight-line strophe of *ottonari*. The metre is used here for the first time, in a movement that gives us a first taste of Roman cruelty and energy.

As a whole the number has the character of an insertion into a ritual ceremony. At a structural level too it therefore highlights the two irreconcilable worlds whose confrontation precipitates the tragedy.

In broad outline Bellini follows Romani's design exactly: twenty-one lines of *versi a selva* are set as recitative; three eight-line stanzas of *settenari* are set as a long narrative *cantabile*; eight further lines of *settenari* in dialogue are set as a *tempo di mezzo*; the eight-line stanza of *ottonari* is set as a cabaletta.

The little prelude to the recitative contrives to combine furtiveness and excitement: the heart-beat style of the opening, the rearing up to a violent *ff* in bars 3–4. The nearest to a definition of the sense of this figure comes later in the scene, when it punctuates the recitative at 'il cor m'agghiaccia'. At the start of the recitative, the idea of darkness and silence is effectively suggested by the long passage of unaccompanied declamation, poised suspended over an implied dominant seventh. Another pictorial touch from the orchestra – extremely modest, no more 'advanced' than in the early or mid eighteenth century – is the plunging scale following 'in lui [the gaping abyss] m'avvento io stesso'; note the grim dissonance and plunging vocal line too. These are vivid, even pantomimic touches. But much of the recitative is confined to a contrast between punctuating chords and sustained, or sometimes *tremolo*, harmonies. The latter invariably accompany Pollione when his thoughts turn to his new love, Adalgisa. A mannerism of Bellini's recitative style is the descending cadence phrase with a strong accentuation (sometimes, actually, a misaccentuation) on the first beat: 'libero è il varco'; 'che il cor m'agghiaccia'; 'la prima fiamma'. Frequent use is made of mediant juxtapositions to surprise, or to underline a change of topic; the richest genuine modulatory passage reinforces Pollione's adoring description of Adalgisa.

The *cantabile* is in fact a '*racconto*': a loose-limbed, narrative aria, in which, in the broadest terms, an A B ab structure matches the three stanzas of the poetry. The A section (as far as Fig. 22) is in itself a fairly typical aria design: a′a″ b c′c″. In the second stanza (VS 34–5), as the narrative becomes more troubled, the structure slackens, becoming a series of short phrases repeated in variation – d d′ e e′ f f′ g g′ – in which, however, the voice and the orchestra are, to begin with, out of phase with one another, and only gradually come into phase:

Orchestra:	3+3 / 2+2 / 1 / 2+2 / 2+2 (link)
Voice: 1½ bars rest, then:	2½+3 / 2+2 / 2+2 / 2+2

The third stanza begins with a part-recapitulation of the first, then evolves through variants of material from both previous stanzas into a coda in which all lyrical poise collapses, and which is cut short by the off-stage sounds of tam-tam and trumpets, starkly summoning the two Romans back to the real world.

The first stanza of the *cantabile* has a processional, quasi-march rhythm and an accompanying orchestral texture that is surely related to those chattering woodwind patterns Italian composers so often used to suggest dreams of love. Bellini controls the melody strictly, not to give away too much too soon: both in the opening line and at 'udia d'Imene i cantici' the unfolding of the melodic contour is quietly paced, even constrained. The scoring is typically generic in quality: strings and horns provide the underlying rhythm, while the woodwind descant is provided by clarinets, oboes, flute and ottavino more or less indiscriminately, depending, that is to say, more on the density required than on any particular colour. But the chromatic appoggiaturas and changing notes lend a sparkling, luminous quality.

The delicious dream vision becomes a nightmare in the second stanza – the music turns to the minor key; a cold mist of *tremolo* obscures the rhythmic shapes; a tentacle-like instrumental theme gropes up from the bass; the easy lyrical style of the singing tightens into sharper dotted rhythms and breaks into declamatory fragments. An additional graphic detail – sanctioned by decades of use in opera

– is the sudden *ff* flash that streaks through the mists and shadows of the orchestral texture at 'folgore'. As with the chattering woodwind in the opening stanza, so too with the 'tentacles of darkness' idea in the second: it is not a particular colour but a specific density that Bellini is aiming for – with the burden of figuration carried by the strings and the *tremolo* harmonies variously sustained by clarinets, trombones, bassoons and horns, the passage shows virtually no sense of the dramatic or poetic potential of orchestral colour.

It is curious to hear Bellini in the third stanza returning apparently unconcerned to the luminous style of the opening at 'Più l'adorata vergine'. But this is soon deflected by the 'gemito' and 'pianto' of Romani's text into the minor key and a touch of graphic detail in the oboe and bassoon. Thereafter the lyrical structure dissolves: the textures of the second stanza return; the nightmare vision of Norma denounces her faithless lover on a monotone, adorned in the orchestra by chromatic appoggiaturas, alternately at her pitch and in the lowest depths, while the harmony creeps chromatically higher until it is cut off by the off-stage tam-tam. In this passage low trombone triads, an octave below the string *tremolo*, do give a real sense of inspissated darkness. Of this movement Lippmann comments, 'since about 1810 Italian composers had composed scenes technically very similar to this dream narration . . . There was in Italy a well-stocked arsenal of musical devices for expressing terror and horror. Nineteenth-century serious opera in Italy learned a hundred times less (if anything at all) from German romantic opera than Weber, Spohr, Marschner and Wagner learned from Rossini, Bellini and Donizetti' (Lippmann 1969, p. 285).

In the off-stage gongs and signals that interrupt the *cantabile*, Bellini sees a cue for basing a substantial part of the *tempo di mezzo* on another Gaulish march, one which will soon be heard in fully developed form in the scene of the mistletoe ceremony. Whereas the march of the druids in the opening scene achieved its sense of expectancy and of waiting in part by being poised on the dominant, this one has much more confidence of purpose, expressed in the rocketing melody, the strutting rhythm, the firm tonic harmony from which it is launched.

Pollione now gathers himself, determined to defy all the supernatural powers that infest these northern forests. This summoning-up of his inner resources demands the use of an orchestral introduction; and the fact that he is so specifically and pointedly defying the powers whose voices we have just heard off-stage prompts Bellini to compose a cabaletta melody that is a kind of 'trumping' of the melody of the druids' march. It has the same marching rhythm, the same vaulting arpeggio shapes, but a more virtuosic elan; in the second half of the theme, as in the second half of the march, the melodic line veers up again and again like a clenched fist. At the end of each quatrain, Bellini breaks the march rhythm with great rhetorical effect, first '*abbandonandosi a piacere*', with a fragrant, vulnerable turn to G minor at thoughts of love, then with an angrily gestic cadence at 'l'empio altare abbatterò'.

Following an opening melodic phrase that emphasizes the mediant very strongly, the aria has a strong modulation to the mediant minor at mid-point. (There is a similar structural reinforcement of the melodically accentuated mediant in the *cantabile*.) It is full of phrases in which the melody (much of it doubled in thirds) simply thrusts its way through, or swings off at a tangent from, the plain underlying chords. As in the *cantabile* the sustaining of the harmony is entrusted largely to violas and bassoons: the glow of woodwind colour that was to become so typical of Verdi's cadences is not found here. A trumpet, as well as the horns, reinforces the strutting rhythm, but even in this aggressive context Bellini lets loose only the woodwind for thematic reinforcement of the singing voice.

No. 3 Scena e Cavatina (Norma)

A setting of I.iii and I.iv of Romani's libretto.

Norma's appearance is described in unusually full and vivid detail, much of it from Chateaubriand rather than Soumet – loose hair, coronet of vervain, golden sickle; she stands on the altar, rolling her eyes like one inspired. The several anticipations of this moment that we have already heard, the procession, the priestly adjuncts, the uncompromising sternness with which she challenges the restless Gauls make this one of the most imposing and authoritative entries in opera. The emphasis laid here and in several other scenes on the need to temper revolutionary fervour with patience has reminded at least one critic that *Norma* was composed shortly after the failed insurrections of 1831.[5]

Although the scene is set by the sacred oak of Irminsul – the 'Nume irato e fosco' who will in due course give the sign that the time has come for blood and revenge – Norma's prayer is addressed to the very different 'chaste goddess', the moon; it is a prayer of peace, not of terror. However, the political connotations of the scene as a whole remain strong – 'eagles' are hated for contaminating the sacred forests and temples; the allusion to Brennus is a good example of those exemplary dips into history to which *risorgimento* writers were so partial (a Gallic equivalent of Hermann the Cheruscan, or of the Battle of Legnano); moral corruption is identified as what really makes great powers vulnerable. In the scene as originally drafted by Romani these connotations dominated the whole number, and even Norma's cabaletta had voiced resentment of the 'perfida gente / Che per pace catene le dà'. The intervention of the censor, if Branca is right (cf. p. 74), made the closing section of the scene less subtle and psychologically true than it might have been. The starting point for her original cabaletta was her agonized recognition that though love had made her a traitress, nonetheless, love was the supreme imperative. The definitive cabaletta is simply the love-song of a woman no longer confident of the devotion of her beloved. Its references would make no sense to us at all if we had not already met Pollione and did not know his feelings.

Norma's cabaletta is an aside; and it is worth underlining its sensational nature: someone who stands at the very heart of a sacred/national community, is indeed the most revered figure in that community, tied into it by vows and by regularly and solemnly enacted ceremonials, is prepared to defy the world, her people, her gods, for the love of a man who is execrated by everyone else she loves, and who himself regards with contempt everything she has hitherto held most dear. The obsession is nicely underlined by the repeated line in her cabaletta ('Ah! bello a me ritorna'), and culminates in the blasphemous hyperbole with which it closes ('E vita nel tuo seno / E patria e cielo avrò').

It is difficult to see that Bellini takes any structural cues from the text in the chorus; he certainly makes nothing of the intoxicating dithyrambic *decasillabi*, and instead of splitting it in the middle as Romani does (four lines description, four lines prophecy), he lays it out in a two-line + six-line structure.

Essentially the architecture is therefore dependent on purely musical contrasts and is carried by the orchestra. The bulk of it comprises the Gaulish march already heard in the *tempo di mezzo* of

Pollione's aria (A and B in the following figure), but this is framed by hymnic solemnities (x, y, z), as follows:

Prelude/	March	/ Prelude + chorus lines 1–2 /	March + chorus lines 3–8 /	Postlude [Prelude var.]
x y etc. /	A A′B Coda /	x z /	A A′B Coda /	x y etc. (link)

Beyond this alternation of 'hymn' and 'march', which might be said to define the poles within which the language of Verdi's 'risorgimental' style was to fluctuate, there is little in the way of dramatic or rhetorical expression. Orchestra and *banda* are both at full throttle throughout the march sections. The prelude uses full orchestra, but when the same material recurs in the central choral x–z section, it has 'priestly' brass only: trumpets, horns, trombones, cimbasso (plus bassoons). In the postlude thrillingly expectant silences replace the drum-rolls of the prelude; one is reminded of Luigi Nono's admiration for Bellini's explosive emptinesses (E. Restagno, *Nono*, Turin 1987, pp. 16–7, cited in Pieri, xxvi).

In broad outline the musical structure of Norma's *scena* and aria corresponds with that of the text: twenty-six lines of *versi a selva* supply the recitative (*scena*); eight lines of *ottonari* + a further two for the chorus provide the material of the *cantabile*; the *ottonari* continue in dialogue form for the *tempo di mezzo* (Romani rarely changed metre at this juncture); and eight + four (*tutti*) lines of *settenari* supply the cabaletta.

During the *scena* Norma's authority is first challenged, then re-established: that process is mirrored in the growing density and then the thinning again of the musical material in which the declamation is embedded. In the opening bars she establishes her ascendancy by shooting out imperious phrases into the silence: they are reinforced by orchestral chords in double-dotted rhythms, coloured by horns and especially trombones. Of the various tension-building *tremolos*, that at Fig. 36 is notable for a menacing figure rising up in the bass, an active, willed counterpart to the sinister stirrings in the bass in Pollione's 'Meco all'altar'.

In the libretto 'Casta Diva' itself is described as a 'preghiera', a prayer. It is preceded by the rituals associated with the sacred mistletoe, which prompt Bellini to provide a long introduction, part harmonic transition and part thematic anticipation. To give the aria even more breadth, he splits the eight lines of Romani's text into two four-line verses, and makes these the outer pillars of a grand ternary design:

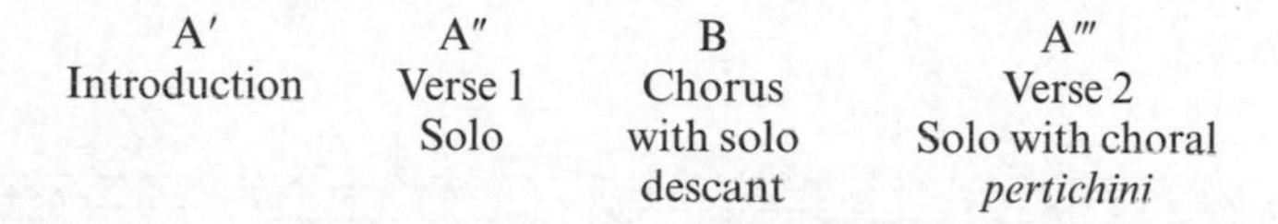

The principal A″ section assumes an X X^{v} y y′ Z form;[6] all the elements except the Z are also used in the instrumental introduction, which serves as the accompaniment to the solemn priestly pantomime. This is one of the rare cases where Bellini gives a specific timbre to his instrumental melodic writing, that of the cool, chaste, sacral flute; the note of pathos at the turn to the minor is deepened by the addition of the oboe.

This classical example of Bellini's '*melodie lunghe, lunghe, lunghe*' is notable for its slow eventuation of the text – the repetitions and ceremonious flourishes suggest some audible equivalent of the solemn gestures and fervent ritual genuflections of a priestly celebrant. Gradually singer and audience alike are drawn into a sonorous ecstasy by the swaying and syncopated rhythms into which the harmony is dissolved, and by the spell cast by the weaving, dipping and vaulting of the soprano line. Soprano as priestess; priestess as ecstatic; and in this combination of functions Norma manages to make the whole cosmos (represented by chorus and orchestra) resonate with harmony, while she holds the vision in focus with her incantatory ululations. Harmonically the aria's interest grows from the protracted, sometimes ornamental and sometimes chromatic appoggiaturas of the X section. These are intensified in y y′, out of which Bellini returns to the tonic with a slow passing-note B♮ that has no real harmonic sense at all; it simply shows the supremacy of line against a dimly apprehended or ambiguous or non-committal background harmony. This tendency comes to a climax in the 'Klangrausch' ('sonorous intoxication' [Lippmann]) of section Z, where a III^7 vi (ex. 4.1) progression is sensuously, caressingly prolonged by triple chromatic appoggiaturas against a pedal A.

In the *tempo di mezzo* the Gauls' march briefly recurs; and from it the dotted rhythms and some melodic inflections are carried forward into the dialogue. The passage provides a striking instance of that fierce reduplication of soloist by chorus that Verdi was to make a feature of his 'risorgimental' style. A curious detail, heard twice, is the chromatic sequence of seventh chords set in a circle of fifths at 'quando il Nume irato e fosco'. It coincides with a sudden drop to *piano* dynamics and must, I think, particularly since it is initially

Ex. 4.1

expressed in *pizzicato*, be designed to impart a conspiratorial frisson to the music.

In a final slower section of the *tempo di mezzo* Norma withdraws into the private world of her own emotions. A minor-key chromatic half cadence provides an effect analogous to that of the eighteenth-century Phrygian cadence between sonata movements in ensuring that, for the cabaletta, F major returns with a real effect of freshness. This withdrawal into reverie requires that the cabaletta too be given an extended instrumental introduction, one that is poised ambiguously between the marching rhythms of so much of the Gaulish music hitherto and the florid raptures into which Norma is soon to fan herself. When she takes up the theme, it is to smooth out the rhythms; the textures are lightened, and she soars, via floated high notes, elegant graces, Chopinesque chromatic coloratura, and '*con abandono*' virtuosity, into a seventh heaven of *bel canto* ecstasy. The cabaletta itself is poised typically between symmetry and exuberant take-off:

A A′	b b′	A→Coda
4+4 bars	2+2 bars	2+7 bars

Particularly effective is the way in which, after the repeat, Bellini suspends the cadential thumpings of chorus and orchestra for little spasms of urgent *cantabile*: 'Ah! riedi ancora qual eri allora'. For these, remarkably, he retained two lines of poetry from an earlier layer of the libretto. (See Chapter 5.)

By now the choral backing no longer matches the mood of the protagonist, and the interstices and the coda are in distinctly different styles from the cabaletta itself; for outside Norma's private dream world the air is still heavy with militarism. As in the cabaletta sung a little earlier by Pollione, a kind of emotional friction is set up between the solo voice in the foreground and the broader musical background against which it is set.

No. 4 Scena e Duetto (Adalgisa, Pollione)

A setting of I.v and I.vi of Romani's libretto.

It is not entirely clear whether Adalgisa stays behind after the mistletoe ceremony, or comes on alone when the rest are gone; probably the latter. But in either case there are two links with what has passed: the last reference, for the time being, to the sacred forest and the rituals that have dominated the opening scenes; and the irony of the fact that here is a shy young girl suffering the same emotional and spiritual dilemma as the imperious Norma.

Lippmann has described this scene as Bellini's 'definitive renunciation of the *sortita*' (Adamo and Lippmann 1981, p. 416). It is a mystery why the composer was not happy with it, for it is surely very fine. It brings into direct conflict the two worlds, Gaulish and Roman, we have as yet experienced only in isolation or alternation; and it does so in a way that is psychologically very telling, in terms of a betrayal (Adalgisa) and a seduction (Pollione). Adalgisa, innocent and idealistic, is battling to keep faith with her gods; everything she says is permeated by her sense of perjury or betrayal. (One notes the contrast with Norma, who long ago has surrendered any will to resist the demands of love.) Where the root of Adalgisa's perjury is her sense of a shameful passion destroying her religious faith, the same conflict, viewed from a different perspective, forms the basis of Pollione's seduction: for he has persuaded himself that he is a faithful lover being destroyed by a cruel god. His style is beautifully matched to the occasion: northern gods are *crudele*, *atroce*, *spietato* (cruel, terrible, pitiless), commanding what their worshippers do not desire, and watching impassively while their hearts are broken. His gods are much to be preferred: why, in Rome, Love is himself a god!

The twelve lines of I.v and the first eleven lines of I.vi are *versi a selva*. Thereafter the whole scene proceeds in *ottonario* metre; moreover, *tempo d'attacco*, *tempo di mezzo* and cabaletta all use the same strophic rhyme-scheme: a.b.a.b.c.d.c.d. The only distinction made between its constituent parts is that, outside the lyrical numbers, the strophes are broken up into dialogue. Not until what we might describe as the 'codetta' or epilogue that follows the cabaletta ('Adalgisa!', 'Ah! mi risparmi') is the pattern varied. There the octave is extended to twelve lines by the inclusion of two rhyming couplets – a.b.a.b.[x.x.y.y.]c.d.c.d. – which underline the most urgent incident in the scene and the fastest exchange in the dialogue, when Adalgisa agrees to elope with Pollione. This long epilogue, protracting the debate far beyond the confines of the set movement, is a striking feature (usually a couple of lines suffice).[7]

The *scena* is preceded by a long prelude which contrives to suggest much – the silence and stillness of the scene; Adalgisa's nervous, tiptoeing entrance; perhaps, in the flute/clarinet cantilena, the voice of a tender passion that keeps calling her back to this place, 'dove a me s'offerse la prima volta quel fatal Romano'; anguish in the cadence phrase, a remarkable succession of incomplete diminished sevenths (=chromatic 6/4 chords).

In both *scena* and duet Bellini reinterprets the poet's scheme in radical fashion. At the close of I.v and therefore halfway through the *scena*, a rhyming *endecasillabo*, 'Deh! proteggimi, o Dio! perduta io son', poignant and ironic, for it is placed immediately before Pollione's entry, is heightened into arioso – almost, indeed, a self-contained little *cantabile*, expanding the brief line of prayer into a lyrical interlude that owes nothing to the structure of the text. Bellini in fact adds words of his own as well as repeating Romani's.[8] An almost romantic warmth (a betraying warmth?) is given by the addition to the string accompaniment of clarinets and, in more modest measure, horns and bassoons. The suspending of the momentum of the scene at this point, the fashioning of the prayer into a complete little ceremony of song, make Pollione's entrance a moment later all the more telling. His interruption of Adalgisa's meditations is reinforced with dissonant, indeed ugly effect: the orchestral figure at the third bar of Fig. 52 is rhythmically brusque, harmonically weird. At 'Ah! t'allontana', Adalgisa attempts in vain to escape from confrontation with him back into the lyrical trance of her prayer.

'Va, crudele' / 'E tu pure', the first of two pairs of regular stanzas that emerge from the long tract of *ottonari*, was presumably designed for a *cantabile*;[9] but Bellini, anxious to express in musical form the conflict in the minds of both characters, breaks the stanzas into what are, in effect, contrasting *tempo d'attacco* and *cantabile* sections: anger v. self-pity in the case of Pollione, passionate despair v. innocent recollection in the case of Adalgisa. The structure is:

Tempo d'attacco	Cantabile
A / B / A^{v} / B^{v} / C (link)	d e d^{v} e^{v} f G . . .
F minor → V	A♭

The metrical continuity of Romani's text stimulates a remarkable musical continuity in the score. There is a suggestion of a cadenza at the end of Adalgisa's verse (as there had been at the end of Pollione's), but instead of a break for applause, the *cantabile* settles into dialogue form (Fig. 57), becomes less formal, and eventually breaks down into recitative. Similarly after the cabaletta: each character sings a solo verse, and these are followed by a *tutti più mosso* much in the customary way. But that does not lead into a duet reprise of the cabaletta; instead Romani's continuing text prompts variants on the cabaletta theme in dialogue, at first free and transitional in character, and only then a full reprise, still in dialogue form. The noisy *più vivo assai* tacked on at the close is the stuff of theatrical routine; but the dissolution of the conventional forms into a fluid musico-dramatic continuity is notable throughout the scene.

The *minore* section of the duet creates a superb image of harshness (Pollione) and pain (Adalgisa) by superimposing a slow declamatory song, full of long appoggiaturas, upon the racing pattern of appoggiaturas and the pulsing chords in the orchestra. It is a *locus classicus* for the magnificent complexity Bellini can create by such means on a foundation of the simplest basic harmonies.[10] The style of the vocal melody is not dissimilar in the *cantabile*, but the mood is transformed by the change in the style of the accompaniment: it is the orchestra that expresses the harsh inexorability of fate, or the gentle pit-a-pat of romantic passion. Both sections of this first movement embody the Bellinian ideal of declamation elevated to the pitch of song.

The cabaletta is slow and tender, laden with dissonant appoggiaturas; especially telling is the false relation at the turn to the minor key, on the words 'del contento a cui ne invita', a delicious example of the tear-laden ecstasy that is so peculiarly Bellini's province. It may be noted that a complete disharmony in the words of the two characters is disguised in the identity of their music: it is the music that tells the truth, in Bellini no less than in Wagner.

Act II (Scene 3)

No. 8 Finale

(a) Scena e Coro

A setting of II.vi and II.vii of Romani's libretto.

The moods of the *scena* are various: self-delusory dreams of love; jealousy of Adalgisa; contempt and fury. But Romani and Bellini chose to focus the scene on the *Coro guerriero*: the definitive discharge of the emotions suppressed in the previous choral scenes. It is one of just two movements in Manzonian *decasillabi* that survive in the opera, and is certainly the better example of their demagogic connotations. Its opening lines echo Chateaubriand, but even in this violent mood Romani's imagery remains predominantly classical – mowing the blades of corn, trimming the eagles' wings.

Branca (1882, pp. 172–4) gives a full account of the problems this movement occasioned with the censors. Their suspicions were neither surprising nor unjustified, for the chorus came to have the same kind of resonance in *risorgimento* Italy as some of the early operatic choruses of Verdi. It was, for example, sung in Palermo cathedral in 1848 to accompany the blessing of the tricolour during a service of thanksgiving for the liberation of Sicily from the Neapolitan Bourbons (H. Acton, *The last Bourbons of Sicily*, London & New York 1961, p. 195). In January 1859 at La Scala *Norma* was removed from the repertory when (for these were the heady months preceding the Third War of Liberation that broke out in the spring) audiences insisted on joining in the singing (Tintori 1983, p. 191). By 1875 the journal *Il pungolo* was describing it as 'the most inspired outburst of bellicose frenzy and patriotic devotion, the one and only rival of the "Marseillaise"' (Branca 1882, p. 174).

It is surprising, even disappointing, to find Bellini doing so little with Norma's last self-deluding dreams of love; there is a sensitive recitative, a few fragments of fragrant orchestral music, but no arioso. So apart from the prelude, the only 'full' music in this scene comes with the chorus.[11]

Once Norma turns from lover to destroyer, nothing is understated, beginning with the shift from string- to brass-accompanied chords, the harmonic wrench and the blood-chilling 'madrigalism' on 'scorreran torrenti'. The summoning of the Gauls is almost shockingly functional. The chorus itself, in its densely-scored (unrelieved, thick *tutti+banda*) and epigrammatic force, yields nothing to the early Verdi in coarseness. 'By heavens', old Zingarelli is supposed to have exclaimed as he read through the score, 'this is *barbarous*' (Florimo 1880–4, vol. III, p. 197). The upward-twisting chromatic appoggiaturas as a symbol of savage aggression contrast vividly with Bellini's customary pathos-laden downward appoggiaturas.

(b) Scena e Duetto (Norma, Pollione)

A setting of part of II.vii and II.viii to II.x of Romani's libretto.

We have not seen Pollione since Act I. What we have heard of him (threatening to ravish Adalgisa from the very altar) does not give us to suppose that he has mellowed in any way. And indeed he reappears cast in the same harsh mould, captured on a suicidal mission, utterly indifferent to his fate – indifferent, at any rate, until Norma discovers that the way to break through his imperviousness is through those he loves: his sons; Adalgisa.

Essentially the scene is another character-study of Norma. At first ablaze with rage and the thirst for revenge, she snatches the knife from Oroveso to kill Pollione. But the sight of him weakens her resolve, and left alone with him the inexorable priestess becomes the all-too-frail woman. Norma's sexual jealousy of Adalgisa has been growing in counterpoint with her friendship for her (cf. II.iii, lines 23–4; II.vi, lines 9ff.), and now becomes briefly the dominating motif of her behaviour: to prevent Adalgisa from winning her lover becomes her first determination. As this ambition fails, both anger and despair mount; paradoxically, but surely very convincingly, the lower she threatens to sink in her degradation, the greater the power she finds she has over Pollione. And gradually her mood swings round; the inhuman cruelty to which she confesses she had almost sunk becomes an inhuman cruelty with which she can threaten and in which she can sadistically exult (II.x lines 18–22, 26–30, 36–40).

In the broadest terms the four stanzas of the duet represent these stages: (i) trying to separate Adalgisa and Pollione; (ii) admitting how close she came, and could still come, to murder; (iii) openly threatening; (iv) (the cabaletta verse) exulting in her power over Pollione.

The whole of this scene, until one reaches the recitative that links into the finale, is in free strophic form. The *cantabile* has two long strophes: 'In mia man' and 'Non sai tu', laid out a.b.a.b.c.c.d.d.e.f.e.f. The 'kissing' rhymes[12] mark the point where Norma breaks away from the dialogue style of the opening to press upon Pollione the urgency of what she is saying: the conditions on which his life may be spared, how close she came to murder. The third strophe is entirely in dialogue, and the 'kissing' couplets reduced to one, where Norma is reminding Pollione of the threat to Adalgisa. The strophic form of the cabaletta is related to the structure of the previous strophes, but reduces them to – as it were – the opening four and the closing two lines. As usual in duets, the first part of the strophe rhymes internally, the last part across the strophes: a.b.a.b.c.d. / e.f.e.f.c.d.

Bellini structures two elements of the *scena* by musical means: a brief processional *parlante* for the leading in of the captive Pollione, and a systematic progression of chromatic modulations as Norma recoils from the idea of killing him. The first of these, with its marching pulse, its off-beat drum rolls, the whimsical cross-string figure of the violins, provides a real theatrical frisson. It is economically but effectively scored, with stalking bassoons to give a dark weight to the bass notes; soft trombones are added at the close. Otherwise, as so often with Bellini, the *scena* is something of a rag-bag of miscellaneous figurations.

The *ottonari* for the *primo tempo* start as soon as Norma and Pollione are left alone at the start of II.x. That Romani intended them to form a *primo tempo* as far as 'ma di lei, di lei pietà' is suggested by their structure, a threefold twelve-line stanza, freely broken up in dialogue between the two voices. This structure is ignored by Bellini, who treats the third stanza and the last two lines of the second stanza as part of a *tempo di mezzo*, while turning the more pathetic dialogue that preceded them into a *cantabile* – a very free and extensive *cantabile*, in which the verse structure is ignored and there is no *a due* singing at all. In the following diagram N=Norma, P=Pollione.

Verse 1 ('In mia man . . .') Verse 2 ('Non sai tu . . .')
Poetry: a b a b c c d d e f e f || a b a b c c d d e f e f ||
N⟶N N⟶N N→N→N⟶
P P P P P P P⟶
Music: a b c d a b c d^{v} E a b c d F g g H I || *tempo di mezzo* ('Ah! crudele . . .')
Key: I I V I VI I

In other words it becomes a kind of double-structured aria, both recapitulatory or rondo-like in certain respects (abcd), yet opening out into a final culmination (HI); at once obsessive and forward-moving, and with episodes that are tonally highlighted in a way appropriate to the mood. After the initial stalemate of wills has been mirrored in the motionless calm of F major for twenty-six long, slow bars, the music opens up to C major as if in a sudden vision of freedom, only to return inexorably to F major as Pollione declines the proffered bargain; as Norma begins to realize that she will fail again, the music turns to D minor and the pace at which the text is delivered accelerates, so preparing for the break into the *tempo di mezzo*. Throughout, the words are magnificently declaimed. Indeed it is one of the opera's sublime examples of declamatory song: it is a melody that loses nothing by being broken up in dialogue, as it is in the opening stanza; words are highlighted by tessitura ('Adalgisa fuggirai'), by rhetorical repetition ('mai più, mai più'), by 'madrigalisms' ('Ch'ei piombi'); the whole is permeated by pathetic appoggiaturas. 'The words are so enmeshed in the notes and the notes in the words that together they form a complete and perfect whole', remarked Rossini (quoted in Florimo 1880–4, vol. III, p. 195). Scherillo (1882, pp. 96–7) links it with the *Adagio* of Beethoven's Septet.

The third stanza of Romani's text ('A me il porgi') is treated not as a single *tempo di mezzo*, but, as is Bellini's wont, as a mercurial series of arioso sections, chief of them a virtuoso *furioso* episode, in which Norma vents her wrath, first in fiercely accented dissonant appoggiaturas, and latterly by the mounting trills. As the aria to follow is to be a cabaletta, not a *cantabile*, Bellini lops off the first two lines of Romani's text as being too statuesquely pathetic and makes them yet another element in the *tempo di mezzo*, this time a recitative, 'Preghi alfine? indegno! è tardi. / Nel suo cor ti vo' ferire'.

The four lines that remain provide material enough only for the very simplest of duet structures. Its affect is the zest and relish of Norma's fury – mirrored in Pollione's retort; this is highlighted at each of the three recurrences of the principal theme, which are preceded by, respectively, a recitative, a poignant arioso, and a strikingly eloquent chromatic close to the *tuttis* that precede the duet verse.

(c) Scena ed Aria Finale (Norma)

A setting of II.ultima of Romani's libretto.

The opera culminates in Norma's recovery of all her most noble and fully human attributes: love – romantic, maternal, filial; self-sacrifice and courage. And in manifesting these qualities Norma simultaneously redeems Pollione and Oroveso, enabling them too to become fully human. The tragic irony of the scene resides in the fact that this moment, transcendental in terms of Norma's humanity, coincides with her utmost humiliation as high priestess: the stripping of her priestly coronet, the black veil, the funeral pyre, the commination. There is no reconciliation here: the Gauls and the woman they had revered as the very incarnation of wisdoms are irredeemably alienated from one another.

The metrical organization of this scene is more complex than anything else in the opera, and especially enigmatic in view of its description as an aria. Nine lines of *versi sciolti* culminate in Norma's confession, 'Son io'; then four lines of *quinari accoppiati* ('Tu! Norma!', 'Io stessa') in urgent dialogue form – the peremptory, snapping effect of the metre is striking – lead into a *primo tempo* or *cantabile* ('Qual cor tradisti') of three eight-line stanzas. The metre changes to *settenari* for a *tempo di mezzo*, in the form of two irregular strophes for the dialogue, and a third strophe for Norma's aria 'Deh! non volerli vittime'. The *quinari accoppiati* recur at 'Padre! tu piangi!' for what looks like a second *tempo di mezzo*, though that is not how Bellini sets it. The last lyrical verses are the eight lines of *ottonari* for the chorus (a.a.b.c. / d.d.e.c.) with a six-line coda for the rest; Bellini's setting superimposes these and the *quinari accoppiati.*

In this finale, as in that to Act I, Bellini's focus on lyricism seems to have been achieved despite pressures to make the scene more spectacular, or more of a *tour de force* for the prima donna, or both. According to Scherillo, 'the impresario advised them to bring the funeral pyre on to the stage and have Norma mount it as she sang a cabaletta finale; but the composer and poet did not accept such an idea, because it would have had a vulgar effect' (Scherillo 1882, pp. 87–8; see also Branca 1882, p. 167). For diplomatic and perhaps commercial reasons the movement is officially entitled 'Aria finale', but Bellini himself described it as comprising 'a concertato and a stretta, both of them so original in style as to reduce to silence any enemies I might have' (Cambi 1943, p. 297).

Initially Bellini follows the structure of Romani's verses closely, setting the nine lines of *versi sciolti* as a recitative *scena*, using the preliminary *quinari accoppiati* ('Tu! Norma!', 'Io stessa' onwards) as a tension-building preparation for the *primo tempo/cantabile*, 'Qual cor tradisti', which materializes as the *quinari accoppiati* fall into stanzaic patterns. The *scena* includes some of the most effectively dramatic harmony in the opera: the tension surrounding the mystery of who is to be the sacrificial victim is skilfully sustained through diminished-seventh-based *tremolos*, which clarify with electrifying effect on a C major 6/4 as Norma offers herself. Rather similarly, the agony of emotion that eventually pours out in 'Qual cor tradisti' is finely excruciated by the chromatic evasion of cadence over nearly twenty bars.

'Qual cor tradisti' is a fine example of a declamatory aria built up out of a mosaic of speech-like fragments rarely more than a bar long. The scoring too is masterly in its understatement: lulling strings for intimacy, rolling timpani for menace – that is all.

In the *tempo di mezzo* Bellini begins to handle the verse more freely, typically breaking down Romani's *settenari* into four stages:

(i) urgent declamation;
(ii) a more extended choral and solo *parlante* based on the 'children's theme' from Act I (the *scena* preceding the first Norma/Adalgisa duet);
(iii) a slower *parlante* for Norma's confession;

(iv) Norma's prayer to Oroveso, set as the first, *minore*, movement of a *cantabile* which continues *maggiore* into the final section of *quinari accoppiati*. Both Hiller and Hanslick see in this finale the model for the Act II finale in *Tannhäuser*. 'One of the best pieces of music that Wagner has written,' opines Hanslick, 'the second finale of *Tannhäuser*, at the powerful climax, "Ich fleh' für ihn", points unmistakably to the influence of this closing scene of *Norma*' (Hanslick 1885).

It is characteristic of Bellini's meltingly lachrymose muse that he should extend Norma's prayer, 'Deh! non volerli vittime', by fusing it into the *quinari accoppiati* of Oroveso's relenting (and indeed the *ottonari* of the choral commentary), to form an extended lyrical climax to the scene. It is constructed on a *minore/maggiore* antithesis during the course of which a tragic declamatory type of song is gradually transmuted into what Lippmann describes as 'Klangrausch'. A transparent, but arresting orchestral texture of sighs and lamentations (graphically rendered by the single notes '*a guisa di lamento*' from a solo horn) pervades the *minore*; the *maggiore* is made up of 'speaking' fragments that can be passed almost naturalistically from voice to voice. But essentially, as Lippmann's oft-made analogy between Bellini and Wagner insists, this is a movement to ravish the hearers by sheer sonorous intoxication. Its swaying rhythms, rising chromatic modulations and ecstatic climactic unison of soprano and tenor voices are erotic in an almost graphic way. In fact it is a supreme demonstration of a fact of Italian opera that is not easily accounted for in rational terms – that not infrequently, in its musical numbers, we are dealing not so much with music drama as with a ritual of communal ecstasy.

The first verse of the choral *ottonari* simply amplifies the sonority of this ensemble. It is not until the second verse, 'Vanne al rogo', that the *ottonari* assume their intended structural function, to form the tragic cadences with which the opera closes. But Romani's carefully fashioned stanzas are treated with scant respect, broken down into exclaimable units, with words and phrases omitted in the urgency of purpose. These bars have the relentless, stark directness and bare functionality of a Verdian close.

5 *A glimpse of the genesis of the opera*

Chapter 1 will have shown that, in one sense, we know very little about the composition of the opera during the autumn months of 1831. In another sense, however, we know a great deal: the autograph score, including many sketches and cancelled sections of music, survives complete, as do many pages of drafts of Romani's libretto. The present chapter provides just a few examples of the kinds of matter that can be illuminated by this material. Space does not permit more than a sampling, and I have chosen to focus exclusively on the opening scene. First, however, it is necessary to describe these manuscript sources:

AL: The autograph manuscript of Romani's libretto, preserved in the library of the Accademia Musicale Chigiana in Siena. Written on paper of a variety of sizes and types, it is a fairly bewildering document, not always easily legible. It consists partly of drafts, partly of alternative versions, partly of fair copies of certain scenes. Some pages contain annotations and alternatives in Bellini's own hand. Plate 3 shows an example: p. 40 of *AL*, in which Bellini's emendations of Romani's text are added partly between the lines, partly in the margins.

A: Bellini's autograph score of the opera, preserved in the library of the Conservatorio di Musica Santa Cecilia in Rome. A facsimile reproduction of this manuscript, with a valuable introductory commentary by Professor Philip Gossett, was issued by Garland in their facsimile series *Early Romantic Opera*. In this chapter I several times refer baldly to 'Gossett': his preface to the facsimile, which is what I am citing, has no pagination; orientation is simple, however, thanks to the movement headings.

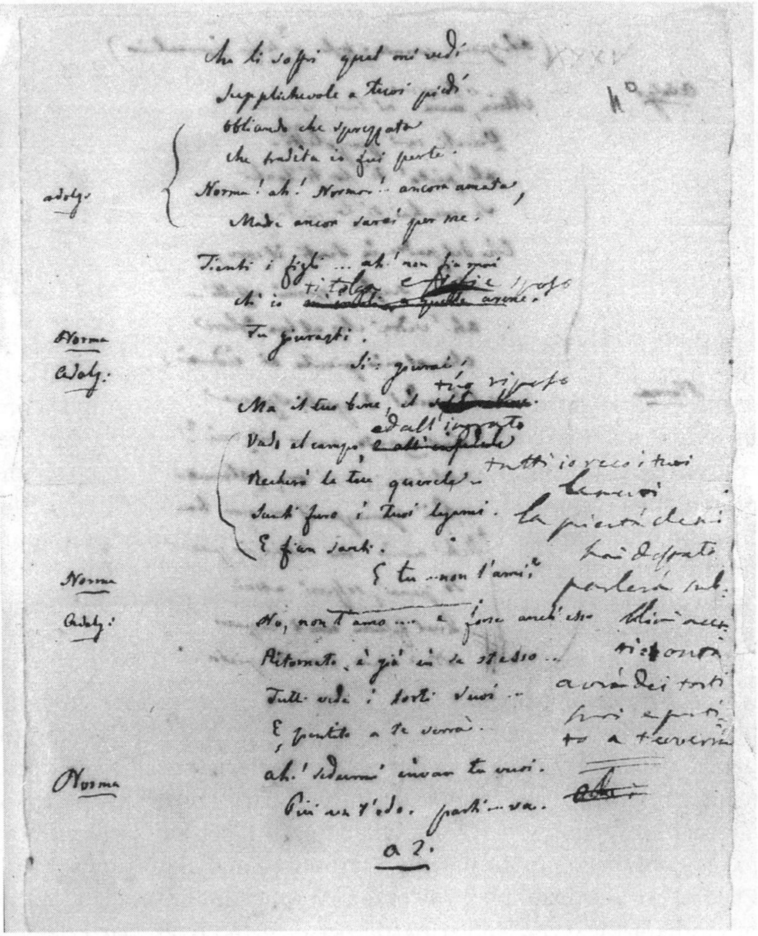
Ah li sospi quel mi vedi
Supplichevole a tuoi piedi
obliando che sprezzata
che tradita io fui per te.
Adalg. Norma! ah! Norma!... ancora amata,
Madre ancor sarai per me.
Tienti i figli ... ah! non fia mai
Ch'io
Norma Tu giurasti.
Adalg. Sì, giurai;
Ma il tuo bene,
Vado al campo,
Recherò le tue querele
Santi furo i tuoi legami.
E fian santi.
Norma E tu... non l'ami?
Adalg. No, non t'amo ... e forse anch'esso
Ritornato è già in se stesso ..
Tutti vedi i torti suoi ..
E pentito a te verrà.
Norma ah! sedurmi invan tu vuoi.
Più nol vedo. parti... va.
a 2.

3. A page of Romani's draft libretto, with autograph emendations and additions by Bellini.

By way of introduction three general comments may be made about *A*:

(i) The composition of *Norma* did not flow effortlessly; as Bellini worked on it, he changed his mind about things over and over again. Some of these changes were points of detail, but many were of a fundamental or long-range kind. Under these circumstances he found himself removing pages and indeed whole groups of pages from his original manuscript and replacing them with new ones.

(ii) From that it follows that the structure of the manuscript is very patchy. Bellini normally composed on bifolios of manuscript paper, and where the composition was going fluently, or where he was in effect making a fair copy of music sketched or drafted in some detail elsewhere, the manuscript comprises a succession of such bifolios. Conversely, a single folio or a sequence of single folios in *A* is a clear sign that first thoughts have been abandoned, that the music has undergone fundamental revision or alteration, or expansion or compression. In the descriptions of the manuscript, bifolios are indicated thus: ⊔; single folios thus: I.

(iii) After the opera had been completed, performed and published, Bellini made a number of alterations in his autograph score in a different, brown ink. These, unfortunately, are rarely distinguishable in the facsimile edition.

S: Sketches survive in some abundance. The greater part of them is to be found in the Museo Civico Belliniano in Catania (CAT), the remainder in New York, either in the Public Library (NYPL), or the Toscanini Collection (TOSC). All this sketch material is reproduced in the Garland score.

It must be said, however, that the blanket term 'sketch' is something of a misnomer. The material in fact belongs to several categories. Some of it is genuine sketch material, thematic ideas jotted down by Bellini, not necessarily with any particular thought of *Norma*. More of it would be better described as continuity drafts. In such material Bellini is composing Romani's text in sequence, laying out the general conception of the scene with voice parts, snatches of instrumental *obbligato*, fundamental bass notes. Quite often these continuity drafts are not preliminary sketches at all: rather they are sections of *A* that have been removed from the main manuscript because Bellini decided, sometimes during drafting, sometimes at the filling-out stage, that they were inadequate to his purpose. Other 'sketches' are in fact fragments of fully worked out and completed composition. Here too we have a case of Bellini simply changing his mind about the effectiveness of something. But in these instances the change of mind came very late in the day, after he had already filled out the details of his continuity draft.

No. 1 Coro d'Introduzione e Cavatina (Oroveso)

AL: p. 1
A: 'Introd: Atto 1, Nr. 1': fos. 14–24 (14–15, 16–17, 18–19, 20, 21, 22, 23, 24)
S: CAT 83–6, 101–2, 58–7, 93–4

AL: There is no fair copy of this scene in the manuscript libretto, and p. 1, which contains most of its material, is not easy to interpret. It is written in three columns, of which the central one consists of five unequal paragraphs of *settenari*, the second, third and fourth of which eventually became the three stanzas of the definitive I.i. Paragraphs one and five were discarded. No characters are named. In the l.h. and r.h. margins are emendations and additions to this central column and first drafts of the following scene between Pollione and Flavio.

A: 'Introd: Atto 1, Nr. 1'. The string of single folios (20–4) show Bellini to have been exercised by two matters in the later stages of the scene: the exact amount of repetition the chorus with solo, 'Dell'aura tua profetica'/'Sì: parlerà terribile', would bear (fos. 20–1), and the timing of the long fade-out with which the movement closes (fos. 23–4).

S: The sketches for this movement are real sketches. In some ways the most intriguing of them is the first (CAT 83). The page is lined up as if for the introductory chorus, with staves for Oroveso, *Coro*, and 'Banda di Fanfarre sul Palco'. The material it contains bears no resemblance to the definitive *Introduzione*, but could very excusably be taken to be a sketch of the Sinfonia, and clearly it is closely related to the opening of the chorus 'Norma viene' (ex. 5.1).

The evidence these materials provide about the genesis of the scene is in fact more mysterious than at first appears. At least three other pieces of information seem to bear on it:

(i) Gossett remarks that the state of *A* fo. 25 (the first folio of the next movement, Pollione's *Recitativo e Cavatina*) suggests that it might at one stage have formed an integral part of the *Introduzione*.

(ii) pp. 9–10 of *AL* contain drafts for what is now the second part of

Ex. 5.1

Norma's cavatina, from 'Fine al rito' to the end of the scene. However, it is headed 'Norma/Atto Primo, Scena Prima'.

(iii) Oroveso's solo scene in Act II is described as his '*sortita*', and was originally designed as a full-scale double-aria; in the event it had to be shortened, allegedly because of Negrini's heart condition.

To those points one might add that, both in structure and in dramatic function, there is a marked resemblance between this opening scene and the scene for Oroveso and the chorus in Act II of the opera.

One might hypothesize wildly about all this, but I offer just a few thoughts. The choice of the term '*sortita*' for Oroveso's Act II *scena* suggests that, as originally conceived, Act I contained no significant solo work for him, or alternatively that the scene that now forms II.iv–v was originally placed early in the opera. I do not think the heading 'Atto Primo, Scena Prima' for 'Fine al rito' can conceivably mean that the action of the opera literally began at that point (cf. Bellini's comment in a letter of 7 September 1831 that he had already sketched an introductory chorus). It is, I suppose, just conceivable that it means: This is a piece of text that belongs to the part of the opera before the first scene change for 'Vanne, e li cela entrambi'; but that would be a most unlikely convention of scene-numbering for Romani to adopt. A more likely hypothesis might be something like this:

At the time Romani began composing his libretto, the opera was intended to open with a large ritual choral scene of which 'Casta Diva' was the culminating item and 'Fine al rito' therefore the first recitative-like passage. When Negrini proved not to be up to the full-scale *sortita* envisaged for him in Act II it was evidently necessary to redistribute the weight of his part, and enhancing his role in the opening scene was the most obvious way of doing that. And as the scene came to assume larger proportions, Bellini and Romani felt the need to enhance its visual qualities, elaborating its processional comings and goings, and in the process making room for Pollione's *sortita* to precede Norma's.

No. 2 Recitativo e Cavatina (Pollione)

AL: pp. 1–2
A: 'Rec° e Cavª Pollione [No.] 2': fos. 25–44 (25, 26, 27, 28, 29, 30–1, 32–3, 34–5, 36, 37–8, 39, 40, 41–2, 43–4)
S: CAT 95–8, TOSC 2

AL: All the libretto drafts for the *scena* are squeezed into the margins of pp. 1–2, which contain the two choral scenes Nos. 1 and 3. The characters are not identified in these early drafts, which are, however, occasionally adorned with drawings of (Roman) heads. The fact that its poetry began life in the form of marginal addenda suggests that Pollione's *sortita* was interpolated within the choral scenes only at a relatively late stage in the planning of the action.

A: 'Rec° e Cavª Pollione [No.] 2'. The structure of the manuscript score shows that it was the recitative that proved particularly troublesome. There were two reasons for that: one was that the *cantabile* 'Meco all'altar' was originally composed in B♭ major; when Bellini decided that it should be in C major instead, the latter stages of the recitative had to be recast. Perhaps more interesting is the interpolated fo. 26: at first the recitative had begun with Flavio's words (slightly different from their final form), 'Troppo t'inoltri! in quella selva è morte', etc. In its definitive form the scene has been expanded backwards, as it were, to provide a commentary on the scenic and acoustic effect of the retreating druids. We have already seen that all the single folios at the close of No. 1. show Bellini to have been working from the other end too, to make this passage as theatrically effective as possible.

S: CAT 95–8 contain the surviving portion of the original B♭ major version of the aria; it is reproduced in Monterosso 1973, pp. 425–30. The closing bars lead directly into fo. 37r of *A*, and since it is completely orchestrated it is clear that Bellini's change of mind came very late in the day. He did not simply transpose the aria, he recast it in various ways and lightened the scoring appreciably. Gossett suggests that it might not have been until he had heard the effect of the aria in the theatre that Bellini decided to change it.

No. 3 Coro – Scena e Cavatina (Norma)

(a) Coro

AL: pp. 2–3
A: fos. 45–51 (all single folios)
S: None

(b) Scena e Cavatina (Norma)

AL: pp. 2, 4–11, 14
A: fos. 52–76 (52, 53–4, 55–6, thereafter all single folios)
(This forms part of No. 3 with no separate numbering)
S: CAT 43–4, 45–8, TOSC 1

AL: The verses for the chorus were written and rewritten over and over again. What Monterosso (1973, p. 431) prints as 'one of the versions' – 'Ella vien: il vento scuote / la disciolta chioma bruna. / Splende al pari della luna / in sua man la falce d'or' – might be described as the first definitive version, arrived at only after much redrafting. After that, two further versions were essayed before Romani decided to turn the chorus into *decasillabi*, originally in the form 'Profetessa terribile a Roma / . . .'

A very substantial proportion of the manuscript is also taken up with drafts and variants of the *scena* and cavatina. P. 2 contains a draft of the first few lines of recitative, 'Sediziose voci'. After that follow on p. 4 drafts for the rest of the scene from 'E fino a quando oppressi' as far as 'Casta Diva', the latter with a multitude of alternative readings, some of them in Bellini's hand; pp. 5–7 then contain a fair copy of the scene so far in a larger hand, with relatively few corrections. This is where the version of the aria text printed by Branca is to be found, though she has omitted two lines (Branca 1882, p. 169). It should read:

Casta Diva, che inargenti	Sia qual balsamo alle genti
Questo suol col vergin volto	Che le piaghe disacerbi,
Nel tenace umor raccolto	Che costanti ancor le serbi
Spandi influssi di virtù.	In sì lunga servitù.

[chorus?] Casta Dea nel sacro vischio
Spandi influssi di virtù.

The definitive version of the text is then written in the l.h. margin, with one difference: lines 5–6 appear as 'Tempra tu de' cori ardenti / Tempra tu lo zelo audace'. It is worth noting that in all the early drafts for 'Casta Diva' the words 'quercia' (oak) and 'vischio' (mistletoe) recur obsessively; neither survives in its final text. Even so, until the cabaletta, every section of the scene makes mention of the forest.

After a blank p. 8, pp. 9–10 contain drafts for the rest of the scene, starting at 'Fine al rito'. It is this draft that is headed 'Norma/Atto Primo, Scena Prima' and quite apart from that tantalizing heading it is one of the most interesting sections of *AL*. It shows that the whole of this *tempo di mezzo* was first drafted in *decasillabi*, of which something like a definitive form emerges in the r.h. column:

Fine al rito, e la sacra foresta / Sgombra ognuno e [a] suoi tetti ritorni / Quando l'ira del Nume sia presto / La mia voce dal tempio s'udra / (Tutti) Ah dall'via (?sul via?) si affrettino i giorni / Altro voto la Gallia non ha.[1]

There then follows what, to judge from the regularity of structure, was designed to serve as Norma's cabaletta. According to Branca this was one of the passages removed from the libretto on the insistence of the censor:

(Tutti ah! tutti tradisco i suoi voti
Profanata, delusa, demente!
Io difendo una perfida gente
Che per pace catene le da.

Dio de' padri, il mio capo percuoti
Se la colpa tu brami punita
Immolarti può Norma la vita
Ma l'amore immolarti non sa.)

Tutti: Valorosi di Brenno nepoti
Soffriam [pur] finche piace al destino
Ma dell'armi il gran giorno è vicino
Ma dell'ire l'istante verrà.[2]

After some preliminary drafting of the Norma–Adalgisa scene I.viii (we are now on p. 10 of *AL*), Romani returned to Norma's cavatina once more, recasting 'Fine al rito' in *ottonari*; p. 11 is a fair copy (much smaller in format than the fair copy of pp. 5–7) and it is this which, in place of 'Tutti ah! tutti tradisco', ends with the cabaletta 'Ah! riedi ancor', quoted by Branca (1882, p. 170), but with a concluding passage for chorus which she does not quote. The full text is as follows:

Ah! riedi ancor / Qual eri allor / Che il cor ti diedi.
Ah! bello ancor / Del primo amor / Al sen mi riedi.
Oblio per te / Onor e fè / Al Dio fo guerra.
Ah! senza te / Non v'ha per me / Nè ciel, nè terra.
Tutti: Sei lento, sì / Bramato dì / Della vendetta
Sei lento, sì / Ma in ciel, non qui / Un dio s'affretta.

Ex. 5.2

Whether or not he had ever set 'Tutti ah! tutti tradisco', Bellini certainly began to compose and almost completed 'Ah! riedi ancor' and some of it survives in *S* (ex. 5.2). For some reason he was dissatisfied with it, went back to the libretto and decided it was the *quinario* metre that was somehow cramping his style. In the margin of p. 11 he wrote '8 versi ottonarj composti degl' istessimi sentimenti di questi 12' (8 *ottonario* lines composed of exactly the same sentiments as these 12). Subsequently, perhaps after Norma's mood of nostalgia had prompted him to recall a likely model for the cabaletta in his own *Bianca e Fernando*, the text was redone once more in *settenari*. This happened probably quite late in the day. Romani's drafts for 'Ah! bello a me ritorna' are on p. 14 of *AL* which is the verso of p. 13 on which is drafted Act II, Scene 4. Curiously, three of Romani's original *quinari* were to survive, slightly altered, to provide text for the coda-like theme on VS 81.1.1f.

Ex. 5.3

A: It is not easy to explain the fragmented state of the manuscript in the chorus. All that can appropriately be said here is that fo. 50 (=VS 53.3.4 to 55.2.2) appears to be a late insertion which has the effect of massively expanding the cadential choral section, while fo. 52 contains a cancelled orchestral epilogue (transcribed by Monterosso: 1973, pp. 431–2).

In the *Scena e Cavatina*, on the other hand, the prevalence of single folios is indeed a symptom of a tortured gestation. Much, but by no means all of this, is still traceable in *A*. I focus on just a few, particularly telling details. At the close of the recitative, 'e il sacro vischio io mieto', the hieratic breadth and nobility of the phrases were achieved only after the rejection of an entirely conventional cadence (Monterosso 1973, p. 432); the A♭ chord on which it closes is then treated as a 'Neapolitan' and, via three detached *pizzicato* chords, the music steps into G major for 'Casta Diva'. There is no trace in *A*, either of the arpeggiated transition or of the decision to transpose the aria into F major.

The final definitive design of 'Casta Diva' was not easily arrived at. At an earlier stage it was more regularly strophic, the second quatrain 'Tempra tu de' cori ardenti' etc.) being set complete as a solo, and the chorus coming in only at the close of the quatrain as in strophe one. There was, however, in this second strophe one moment of strikingly greater intensity, when the harmonies underlying the climactic bar of syncopated high Bs (as in VS 68.1.2) were boldly reharmonized (ex. 5.3). There was also a florid coda, transcribed by Monterosso (1973, p. 434). In due course Bellini decided that the intensification he had achieved in the second strophe could be achieved in a more concentrated form by dovetailing the solo and choral sections, so that in its latter stages, 'spargi in terra' etc., Norma's song is supported and coloured by the choral sonority.

Ex. 5.4

A also contains the remains of a different *tempo di mezzo*, again transcribed in part in Monterosso (1973, pp. 435–6). I quote its final bars (ex. 5.4) to show how it links up with the original cabaletta. The original tonal scheme, from a G major cantabile to an A♭ major cabaletta (see below), was obviously radically different from that with which we are familiar, where both arias are in F major.

S: The Catania 'sketches' are in fact relics of the original layer of *A*, removed when Bellini decided that the aria was not working. CAT 43–4, which followed directly on from fo. 66 of *A*, contains the start of the cabaletta, complete in every detail (see ex. 5.2); CAT 45–8, in part printed by Monterosso (1973, pp. 437–8),[3] contain the transition into the cabaletta repeat. By this stage Bellini was losing interest, and he never completed the orchestration.

No. 4 Scena e Duetto (Adalgisa, Pollione)

AL: pp. 15–17, 26–9

A: 'Duetto per Adalgisa e Pollione Norma Nr. 4': fos. 76–100 (76–7, 78–9, 80–1, 82–3, 84–5, 86–7, 88–9, 90, 91–2, 93, 94, 95, 96, 97, 98, 99–100)

S: CAT 113–16, 1–8, 9–10, 11–20, NYPL 1–4, CAT 29–36, NYPL 5–6, CAT 21–2, 23–4, 69–78 (71–2, 69–70, 75–6, 74–3, 77–8)

AL: pp. 15–17 contain the fair copy of I.v and I.vi. A few jottings at the foot of p. 17 suggest that at one point Romani considered adding a cabaletta (which would have presupposed that he was at first thinking of 'Va, crudele' as the *tempo di mezzo* and 'Vieni in Roma' as the *cantabile*. On p. 26, which must at some stage have been sent to Bellini by post or messenger, there is a note which refers both to this movement and the following (or the Act II) duet for Norma and Adalgisa. Romani writes, 'I enclose the alterations for the duet of the two women; for that of the tenor and Grisi I don't remember what you said to me. We'll see one another at the Cafe. R[omani]'. Whatever it was, however, that Bellini said to Romani at the café must have been insufficiently lucid or definitive. The scene had a more tormented genesis than any other part of the opera. It will not be helpful for our purposes even to attempt to describe the draft material on pp. 27–9. Weinstock reports that seven complete versions of the text have been claimed to survive (1972, p. 488). My own impression of these pages, however, tallies rather with Monterosso's description: 'one is confronted with a most intricate confusion, to the point where it is virtually impossible to unwind the tangled skein of lines scarcely sketched in, lines cut off half way, ideas in two ill-matching couplets, or in couplets which don't match at all, variant readings squeezed between the lines, and so on' (Monterosso 1973, p. 454).

A: 'Duetto per Adalgisa e Pollione Norma Nr. 4'. Bellini's confession that, even after the opera had been completed and successfully performed, this movement left him unsatisfied, certainly should not be taken to mean that his conscientiousness had failed him, or his energy flagged. This is 'the single section of *Norma* for which the greatest number of preliminary drafts exists' (Gossett); and the straightforward structure of the earlier part of the manuscript is due to the fact that, after abandoning so many preliminary drafts, Bellini was able to make of it a kind of fair copy. Not that the copy is particularly fair; even after finalizing the form and content of the scene he continued to worry over details, some of them quite fundamental. The definitive form of the violin part in the *tempo d'attacco* 'Va, crudele' has had to be pasted in over whatever it was Bellini had previously imagined; and at some stage he had second thoughts about the keys or pitch of the music. On fo. 76r he has noted that the music should be 'in B major with five sharps'; fo. 84r, where 'Va, crudele' begins, also has a note suggesting transposition upwards to F♯ minor/A major. In the cabaletta all those single folios betray Bellini's

4. Pollione (Stefano Algeri) and Adalgisa (Katherine Ciesinski) in their Act I duet; Scottish Opera production 1992/3 (photograph Bill Cooper).

difficulties in determining exactly how the pattern of statements, counterstatements and dialogues should be organized. The musical examples in Monterosso's article (1973, pp. 455–7) – from fos. 93–7 of *A* – show that even the principal theme of the cabaletta assumed its familiar form only very late in the day.

S: For a study of Bellini's methods of sketching, drafting and revising, this duet provides an exceptional wealth of material.

CAT 111–16 contain sketches for the instrumental prelude. In view of the indecision about key mentioned above, the most interesting detail is the fact that the sketch is in C major.

CAT 1–10 contain a continuity draft of the *primo tempo*, which Gossett suggests may well have been the first layer of *A*, following on directly after fo. 83v. Pollione's strophe runs down to the end of CAT 8, at which point there is a lacuna before the major-key part of Adalgisa's strophe begins at '(Il pensiero al cielo er)gea'. This sketch is transcribed in Monterosso (1973, pp. 441–3). Already Bellini's conception of the movement is quite clear: a declamatory minor-key setting of the first few lines, and a more lyrical and ultimately florid major-key setting of the last four. What startles us about this sketch is that the music is familiar from a quite different context. Both minor-key and major-key sections, instead of being gradually refined into the definitive version of the movement, were subsequently removed and transferred to form the stretto of the Act I finale, 'Vanne, sì, mi lascia, indegno'.

CAT 11–20 (transcription in Monterosso: 1973, pp. 445–7). In the new *minore* opening Bellini has found the seed of the definitive form. A bar of violin figuration on CAT 16 links Pollione's verse with Adalgisa's exactly as in the final form of the duet (VS 97.4.2) and may suggest that he already had some idea of the energetic instrumental style against which the declamation was to be set. On the other hand the *maggiore* theme of this draft subsequently disappeared without trace.

NYPL 1–4, CAT 29–36, NYPL 5–6 (transcription of CAT 29–36 in Monterosso: 1973, pp. 448–50). In Gossett's words, 'though these pages are separated by an ocean, they belong to a single layer of Bellini's work, preserving the entire opening section of the *Duetto*, almost up to the beginning of the cabaletta, in a draft that may well have immediately preceded the final version of the autograph. The opening is a further refinement of the F minor phrase we know from the second version (i.e. CAT 11–20); the major section presents still another theme, this one ultimately placed in [Norma and Pollione's Act II duet at] "Già mi pasco ne' tuoi sguardi"'. In other words the 'Sol promessa al Dio tu fosti' theme is the theme we have already met as the lyrical, major-key element in the Sinfonia. And Gossett questions the traditional (Bellini's own) account of the Sinfonia because when the theme appears in these duet sketches it is not taken up as something pre-existent and ready-made, rather as something that Bellini is still working on. He hasn't yet resolved the question of

Ex. 5.5

whether the first full bar should consist entirely of repeated notes, and he hasn't decided what kind of rhythmic spicing the second bar needs. It begins as a row of regular crotchets; then he adds a crotchet to turn the second half of the bar into a triplet; ultimately in the Act II duet he will syncopate it (ex. 5.5). But that ultimate state had already been achieved in the Sinfonia.

The NYPL pages are authenticated as genuine Bellinian autographs by Bellini's brothers Mario and Carmelo ('Autografo di Vincenzo Bellini e i suoi fratelli Mario Bellini e Carmelo Bellini'). NYPL 1 shows that the definitive violin figuration had already been worked out – another curiosity, in view of the fact that in *A* it had to be pasted in as if it were a last-minute idea

CAT 21–4 (transcription in Monterosso: 1973, pp. 450–1). Still unresolved on the theme for the major-key half of his *tempo d'attacco*, Bellini made two further attempts. Gossett suggests that, since both take up at the point where *A* fo. 85r breaks off, that is to say VS 95.2.3, they may be 'closely tied to the actual writing of the autograph'. I take that to mean that, as Bellini was making what he had intended to be the fair copy of this scene, he was again overwhelmed by doubts and broke off to make further sketches. Nothing came of the first sketch; the second (CAT 23–4),based on the *Ernani* sketches of the previous year, became in due course Oroveso's Act II aria 'Ah! del Tebro al giogo indegno'. By this time then, Bellini had written five different themes for the words 'Sol promessa al Dio tu fosti' etc., none of them really persuading him that it was absolutely right. And so, 'the composer admitted defeat, gave up all thought of further attempts and turned to a theme borrowed from the *aria di camera* "Bella Nice, che d'amore" composed a few years earlier in 1829' (Monterosso 1973, p. 451).

CAT 69–77 contain sketches for 'Vieni in Roma, ah! vieni, o cara'. They need to be read in the order 71–2; 69, 70; 75 (76 is blank); 74, 73; 77. The prevarication evident in *A* does not demonstrate that Bellini had done less thorough preparatory work for this cabaletta. These draft pages in fact show him already getting his teeth into precisely the problems that were to prove so intractable right down to the final stages of composition. CAT 71–5 consist of a first, continuity draft, following on directly from fo. 94v of *A* (VS 104.5.3) with the last note of Pollione's strophe, followed by Adalgisa's and a transitional link into the dialogue-like reprise 'Qui domani all'ora istessa' etc. This transitional link, which included nothing resembling the present *più mosso*, breaks off on CAT 75 when Bellini decided it needed to be treated more expansively. CAT 74, 73, 77 contain this expanded transition. Monterosso's transcription shows how it links up with CAT 69, 70 (1973, pp. 457–9). Agonizings over the movement's overall structure continued into *A*, where for the first time the idea of a *più mosso* occurs (fos. 96r–97r). Having hit upon this, 'Bellini decided to return to the shorter sketch, CAT 75, as his model for the remainder of the transition' (Gossett).

6 *Some variant readings*

An equal but different interest attaches to the variant readings in the first printed edition of *Norma*, a vocal score issued in the spring of 1832: *NORMA / Tragedia lirica di F. Romani / posta in musica e dedicata / Al Signor / N. ZINGARELLI / dal suo allievo / V. BELLINI / Riduzione per Canto con acc.to di P. F. . . . NAPOLI – MILANO / TITO DI GIOVANNI RICORDI* (plate nos. 3723–3736).

There can be no doubt that, except for the few minor errors it contains – missing accidentals etc. – this was the form in which, at the time, Bellini expected and wished for his opera to appear. Yet in several movements it differs fundamentally from the modern vocal score (plate no. 41684), the readings of which go back to Ricordi's second edition of *Norma*, 'corrected in accordance with the last modifications carried out by the author' (plate nos. 30981–30995) (Brauner 1976, p. 108). The purpose of the present chapter is to scrutinize those changes that affect the structure of the opera, and to argue that, in general, the original versions are superior.

***No. 5* Finale (Act I)**

(a) Scena e Duetto (Norma, Adalgisa)

The original vocal score (plate no. 3729) published the cabaletta in a different form: between Norma's solo verse and what does service for the duet verse. Adalgisa too had a solo verse, essentially identical with Norma's solo, except for the text. There followed an entirely conventional linking passage: a bar of overlapping dialogue (performed three times), and two bars of cadenza *a due*, leading into the duet verse. For the most part this was the same as the revised version's duet verse, but with the roles reversed. One or two passages had been different, however: Norma's little coloratura spasm at 'al caro oggetto *unita*' was bolder and more angular in its flourish, and there was nothing in this version to match her exultant high pedal note on 'vivrai'. Instead Adalgisa had been gradually drawn into Norma's coloratura, which needed accordingly to take a slightly simpler form than in the second version. The cadenza was not altered.

Is the familiar version in the later edition to be preferred? It certainly allows the music to move forward more urgently to the peripeteia of the following recognition scene; and there is no worthwhile musical invention that is sacrificed by the cut. Nevertheless, I am not sure that the full-length version is not more persuasive.[1] There is surely something a little unconvincing in Norma's having to play second fiddle to Adalgisa in the duet verse simply because Adalgisa has been deprived of her solo. Nor could the situation be rationalized psychologically by suggesting that Norma is, as it were, sinking back into the introspective musing in which she began the *cantabile*; her role in the cadenza puts that out of court. Nor could it be corrected by restoring the leading role in the duet verse to Norma: for that would be to reduce Adalgisa's role in the cabaletta close to insignificance, and it is, within the constraints imposed by the relationship between the two characters, Adalgisa's scene.

(b) Scena e Terzetto (Norma, Adalgisa, Pollione)

At the premiere this was one of the numbers that was not well received (see review quoted on p. 14). Some months later, however, at Bergamo, Bellini singles out this finale as having been particularly effective, and in doing so seems to imply that he had made no concessions to popular taste to achieve this effect (see letter quoted on pp. 7–8). Branca seems to provide further confirmation of this claim when she writes, 'since it didn't fit the action, Felice Romani, who in other works had emancipated himself from the pressures of the stage, and who aspired to free opera entirely from convention, flatly refused [to bring back the druids]' (1882, p. 167). It is not easy, however, to relate these descriptions to the two versions of the finale which are preserved. And since Florimo and Branca, even in harness, are not the most reliable of witnesses, the best policy will be simply to give my own account of how the first edition (still plate no. 3729) differs from the familiar one in currently available scores.

First: In the *cantabile* 'Oh! di qual sei tu vittima' the curiously deformed effect which the movement usually gives is readily understood when one sees that it was designed as a regular canonic movement; it has been crudely pruned by removing the seventeen bars of Adalgisa's verse, and with them some of her text and some of its sense. There can be little doubt of the superiority of the first version. For one thing it works out its musical idea with a far more satisfying sense of clarity, spaciousness and completeness – it is, after all, the emotional working-through from the opera's recognition scene, and there is absolutely nothing being held up by giving it in full. For another, the removal of Adalgisa's verse reduces the movement to what is essentially a confrontation between Norma and Pollione, while the object of the confrontation (Adalgisa herself) is reduced to the role of bystander. Furthermore, it loses one of the rather nice psychological points of the original: Norma's solo, at once grave, admonitory and insinuating, lays out Adalgisa's dilemma; thereafter, in the full canonic form, her two verses of *pertichini* enable her to contrast her solicitude for Adalgisa (by singing in supporting harmony with her) and her disgust for Pollione (by punctuating his verse with explosive declamatory outbursts). The revised version gives a non-committal impression of a canon in which the composer has lost interest; and the length of the *a tre* epilogue (twenty-two bars) is disproportionate to the length of the thematic exposition (thirty-three bars).

Second: In the later editions the stretta 'Vanne, sì, mi lascia, indegno' has been cut back even more drastically, but also expanded (and this is where Bellini's comments after the Bergamo performance obfuscate rather than illuminate) by the inclusion of the off-stage effects of gongs and druids' chorus.

The original was designed as a kind of cabaletta *a tre*, of strikingly original and curious cast. In essence the verses of the cabaletta each assume the same form as in the revised version:[2]

A	4 bars	Tonic (A)
B	4+2 bars	Tonic → Dominant (b b′ x)
C	4+4 bars	Dominant preparation (c c′ y z)
D	[4]*+8+2 bars	Maggiore (D′ D″ d‴)

The lack of the usual poised thematic symmetry in B, and the irregularity of the phrasing remains striking even in the revised form. But whereas, in this revision, the other singers merely exclaim 'Ah!' during the orchestral link (z) into the *maggiore*, the original design entailed the extraordinary feature of Pollione's interrupting Norma's verse with an anticipatory rendering of D′ (* in the diagram), so that the major-key section was fourteen bars in length.

There had followed a solo verse for Pollione, which Adalgisa interrupted at the turn to the major, and a solo verse for Adalgisa which Norma and Pollione interrupted, singing together in octaves. During Adalgisa's verse, however, both Norma and Pollione had contributed *pertichini* at phrase ends. At the end of Adalgisa's verse, overlapping phrases for Norma and Pollione press upon one another, as in the modern vocal score (VS 153–4). A further striking difference in the original edition is that the styles of accompaniment figuration are matched to the characters: the women both had an agitated 𝄿♩♫ pattern, which gave way to sweeping triplets in the *maggiore*; Pollione had a tense ♫ 𝄾 ♪ ♫ repeated chord pattern throughout both *minore* and *maggiore*. Except for the addition of the chorus and a speeding-up of the cadential harmonies (at VS 157), the codas are identical in substance.

A few moments of time have been saved by these changes; but except for the off-stage *coup de théâtre* at the close, which entails no new music at all, it is difficult not to feel that here too the revisions have denatured the highly individual qualities of the original conception. As in the duet with Norma, Adalgisa has again been downgraded: no dramatic or psychological, still less musical or poetic, purpose is served by having her sing her verse as a second part accompanying Pollione. The carefully calculated distribution of the singers has been destroyed, the climax now coming, not with the overlapping piling-in of phrases as in the original, but with the crudely vehement *a tre* octaves of VS 151f.; the carefully calculated variety of instrumental figurations has become a random confusion of alternatives, taken up and dropped again for no clear reason.

From the first, this Act I finale was a problem. At some stage Bellini seems to have lost confidence in it, and was moved to trim it drastically, making its excitements faster to arrive and grosser in the savouring. Now that *Norma* is a well-loved work, and audiences are more tolerant of expansive scores than they were in early nineteenth-century Italy, it would be opportune to reinstate the evidently superior original readings, as has long been the custom with the Act II war-hymn.

No. 6 Introduzione (Act II)

In the first edition of the vocal score (plate no. 3730) the prelude was more extensive: the lyrical melody was played twice, once as we know it now, as a mournful cello *cantabile*, the second time in octaves by the treble instruments. If minutes are precious, this is a cut that might be allowed to stand: at least the movement is not rendered obscure or denatured as a result of it. On the other hand the proportion of expressive *cantabile* to merely incidental music, however vivid, is significantly changed, and it may be doubted whether the minutes saved will be better spent than they would have been in listening to this sombrely magnificent passage in new colours.

No. 8 Finale (Act II)

(a) Scena e Coro

This movement, uniquely, is not an integral part of the autograph score but an insertion in the hand of a copyist. It corresponds entirely with the version of the chorus in the modern vocal score. A profusion of autograph sketches and continuity drafts show that Bellini did not easily decide on a definitive version.

The first edition of the vocal score (plate no. 3734) contains two alternative versions: that familiar from the modern vocal score, and one closing with a *maggiore* coda on which, in due course, one imagines, the coda of the *Sinfonia* was to be modelled.[3] This is the one movement in the opera where modern performances, following the example of Gino Marinuzzi (Tintori 1983, p. 192), have commonly abandoned the later edition of the movement and reinstated an earlier reading, or at least a reading that occurs as an alternative only in the earlier printed edition of the vocal score.[4]

One curious and thought-provoking feature of the first edition is that, even in the version of the chorus that is musically identical with that in the modern edition, the poetic text is different:

Guerra, guerra, le Galliche selve Quante han quercie producon guerrier. Quai [*sic*] sui greggi fameliche belve Sui Romani van' essi a cader.	= VS 214.4.1–215.2.5
Strage, strage, esterminio, vendetta! Già comincia, si compie, s'affretta Come biade da falci mietute Son di Roma le schiere cadute Tronchi invanni [*sic*], recisi gli artigli, Abbattuta ecco l'aquila al suol.	= VS 216–17
Strage, strage, esterminio, vendetta! Abbattuta ecco l'aquila al suolo, Come biade da falci mietute Son di Roma le schiere cadute A mirare il trionfo de' figli Viene il Dio sovra un raggio di sol.	= VS 218–220
A mirare il trionfo de' figli Viene il Dio sovra un raggio di sol.	*maggiore* coda; not in VS

It thus transpires that what the current libretto curiously labels 'II' – the four lines 'Sangue, sangue' to 'con funebre suon', a second quatrain matching the opening quatrain 'I' – does not appear in the original edition at all. They are, it will be noted, the most bloodthirsty and vicious lines in the chorus, and might have been added (one hypothesizes) when the visionary coda was cut. What is quite clear is that this shorter text fits the shape of the music – A bA bA Coda – appreciably better. The major-key element of the episode b coincides with the exclamation 'Strage, strage'; the reprise of A is matched to a textual repetition: 'Come biade da falci mietute'; and of course some structural and expressive point is made of the vision of victory. In the revised edition, the implied parallelism of verses 'I' and 'II' is not matched in the music, and verse 'III' enters in the middle of a musical period – coincides, in fact, with the answering phrase of the second appearance of A.

So one has two alternative versions of this chorus: an optimistic, visionary one, with its emphasis on the 'Dio sovra un raggio di sol', and its consistent reinforcing of the poetic structure by the musical structure; and the version of mere destructive hatred, which has an additional verse of text that throws the matching of poetry and music out of balance, and which cuts the luminous coda.

7 *Contemporary reactions to 'Norma'*

After the second performance of *La straniera* in February 1829, the *Gazzetta privilegiata di Milano* had remarked: 'Amid the irruption of the Rossinian torrent, it is no small thing that a young composer should signal the first steps in his career by attempting a genre that could be called new for the present period. Not only is he the restorer of Italian music, but also – a modern Orpheus – he has resuscitated the beautiful melody of Jommelli, of Marcello, of Pergolesi, with beautiful song, with splendid, elegant, pleasing instrumentation' (quoted in Weinstock 1972, p. 66).

Bellini enjoyed a notably successful career; of his ten operas only *Zaira* and *Beatrice di Tenda* failed to receive the most enthusiastic welcome from his contemporaries. As these comments on *La straniera* show, however, he was widely, and surely correctly, perceived as stepping aside from the mainstream of modern Italian music, so brilliantly represented by Rossini. To do that was to be, in some measure, controversial. Bellini's operas, particularly those produced in Milan, the spiritual centre of the Romantic movement in Italy, excited debate in a way that Donizetti's operas, or even Verdi's earlier operas, rarely did.

Togn and Pepp

We may begin with one of the most unusual tributes ever paid to an opera. Within a few weeks of the premiere, Carlo Angiolini, a Milanese dialect poet, published *La Norma resiada* (*The Norma Debate*), in the form of a 'dialogh tra el Scior Togn e tra el Scior Pepp' (Dialogue between Signor Tonio and Signor Peppino). The two men are good friends, but 'so different in our tastes and our way of thinking that . . . even in paradise we shall go on squabbling'; for Pepp is a Rossinian, while Togn has fallen under the spell of Bellini, and they debate their enthusiasms through thirteen pages of racy Milanese dialect. They do not fail to cross swords on the controversial matter of the (Act I) finale: for Pepp, 'Bellini is really not much of an artist, or if he is, he still has to show it. He still has to write a really good finale, a proper concertato piece like *Otello*, or like the quartet in *Bianca e Faliero*, in *Demetrio* and *L'Italiana in Algeri*.' 'Does one have to be so pedantic,' retorts Togn; 'does one always have to finish in the same style? Isn't it a fine thing to strike out on a new path? You, Pepp, are the only one who doesn't approve.'

It was a matter of temperament too: 'What has Bellini ever done with real flair? It's not his fault that he doesn't have the genius and has to try so hard; but why ever do the papers praise him to the heavens? Perhaps because the ladies find him *simpatico*, and just at present the ladies' fashion is all for the sentimental . . . Even when there is absolutely nothing to weep about, they are so serious, so melancholy, they are like a troop of Madonnas of the Seven Sorrows.' Bellini, replies Togn, is like a painting by Titian, compared with a poster by Moncalvo, and of course there are 'some who like those red and yellow puppets, hunchbacks and dwarfs . . . But a man of feeling, a man with a true heart, enjoys a tragedy as much as he does the best of comedies.'

Mazzini and Schopenhauer

We must imagine Togn and Pepp debating the merits of *Norma* in the streets of Milan. The questions that exercised them, however, also interested other very different kinds of men, working in very different arenas – even contemporary philosophers. There could hardly be a mental contrast more sharp than that between Giuseppe Mazzini, political philosopher and activist, one of the chief architects of Italian nationhood and independence, and Arthur Schopenhauer, in whom the philosophy of transcendental idealism came to its pessimistic and misanthropic culmination. Both found in *Norma*, which they knew well, food for philosophical reflection, though inevitably the insights they derived from it could scarcely have diverged more radically. The Mazzini passage is from his *Filosofia di musica* of 1836; the Schopenhauer from 'Zur Ästhetik der Dichtkunst', Chapter 37 of the second, supplementary volume of *Die Welt als Wille und Vorstellung*, added to its 1844 edition.

Giuseppe Mazzini

Bellini, whose premature death we lament, was not, it seems to me, a progressive genius; and had he lived he would not have extended the limits within which his music revolved. Virtually the whole of the last act of *Norma*, conceived and designed in a Raphaelesque spirit, contains all of Bellini.

Though superior to all the others who are imitators of imitators, Bellini was a transitional genius; a link between the Italian school as we have it today, and the school of the future; a melancholy voice between two worlds; resounding with memory and desire. Like the exiled Peri, he wandered to the gates of a paradise where he had no hope of entering. His music – when it doesn't resemble Metastasio's sickly-sweet languor – resembles the poetry of Lamartine! a poetry which invokes the infinite and aspires towards it, but prostrate and with prayer: a poetry that is sweet, amorous, pathetic, but resigned, submissive, and in the long run more inclined to enfeeble, to enervate, and to make sterile the power of the human spirit than to strengthen it, to revivify it and to make it more fruitful . . . But today, in order to bring about a revival in literature and in music it is necessary, for anyone who aspires to a position of leadership, to combine the power of Byron with the active faith of Schiller. Bellini's music lacks both. You might say that he drowned himself in his music, moved perforce by some inner presentiment of his premature fate, and that this presentiment prevented him, with rare exceptions, from rising to daring conceptions. (*Edizione nazionale degli scritti di Giuseppe Mazzini, Vol. VIII*, Imola 1910, pp. 158–9)

Arthur Schopenhauer

And here let it be remarked that the real tragic effect of the catastrophe, that is to say the hero's resignation and exaltation of spirit that the catastrophe brings about, rarely appears so purely motivated and so clearly pronounced as in the opera *Norma*. It comes about in the duet, 'Qual cor tradisti, qual cor perdesti', in which the reversal (Umwendung) of the Will by the sudden setting in of calm in the music is clearly marked. Altogether, this work – quite apart from its magnificent music, and quite apart too from the poetic diction, which can be nothing more than that of an opera libretto – simply in consideration of its subject matter (Motiven) and its inner organization is a tragedy of extreme perfection, a true model for tragic design of a theme, tragic progress of a plot, and tragic denouement. And the effect it has on the hero's state of mind is that of raising him up above the world, an effect which passes over on to the spectator. Indeed, the effect achieved here is so much the more natural and more characteristic of the true nature of tragedy in that no Christians and no Christian sentiments appear in it.

The German Romantics

Wagner

Among his fellow Italian composers Bellini had by now won for himself a unique position: Rossini, Mercadante, Donizetti, Pacini, the Ricci brothers, all viewed his mature operas, *Norma* in particular, with admiration and love. Tradition attributes a role to *Norma* in Rossini's permanent and Pacini's temporary retirement from the theatre.[1] In Germany matters were less straightforward. German composers had always been engaged in a creative exploration of other musical traditions, particularly perhaps, the Italian; but the best composers of the Romantic generation took different views on how far this was still possible.

Nevertheless, for our purposes, a special interest attaches to the writings of at least one of these young German Romantics. Richard Wagner's years of apprenticeship as an operatic conductor coincided with the spread of Bellini's reputation to the furthest corners of Europe and beyond. He experienced the Bellini fever that hit Leipzig in the spring of 1834 in the wake of Wilhelmine Schröder-Devrient's appearance there as Romeo in *I Capuleti e i Montecchi*, and this opera and *La straniera* were both in the repertory that he conducted in Magdeburg between 1834 and 1836. At Königsberg in 1836–7 he extended his acquaintance with Bellini to include *Norma* and *I Puritani*; and in his first season at Riga (1837–8) he conducted ten performances of *I Capuleti e i Montecchi* and eight of *Norma* (J. Warrack, in P. Burbidge & R. Sutton (eds.), *The Wagner companion*, London 1979, p. 92). In the essays written during these years Bellini is ever-present. There exist few more eloquent accounts of the art of *bel canto* than those from the hand of the young Wagner, and few more shrewd diagnoses of what is required of singers who aspire to perform Bellini.

In later years Wagner was understandably less concerned with the operatic repertory that had dominated the theatres in his youth. Nevertheless Bellini remained 'one of the few composers about whom Wagner never made negative critical comments' (J. Kühnel, in U. Müller & P. Wapnewski (eds.), *Wagner Handbook*, Cambridge, Mass., 1992, p. 567) and the occasional tributes he continued to pay are remarkable for their generosity. In August 1872, Cosima notes in her diary, 'Richard sings a cantilena from *I Puritani*, and remarks that Bellini wrote melodies lovelier than one's dreams' (J. Malte Fischer, *Ibid.*, p. 529). It was Schröder-Devrient as Romeo, he told her in March 1878, who lay behind the 'rapturous extravagance' ('Ueberschwänglichkeit') of Act II of *Tristan und Isolde*.

Wagner's most intensive occupation with *Norma* occurred in the years 1837–9. On 11 December 1837 he chose the opera for his first Riga benefit performance. In readiness for this he undertook a certain amount of orchestral retouching of Bellini's score (WWV 46) – essentially modifications in the wind parts, made less to 'improve' Bellini's orchestration than to adapt it to the capabilities of the Riga orchestra (J. Deathridge, M. Geck & E. Voss (eds.), *Wagner Werk-Verzeichnis: Verzeichnis der musikalischen Werke Richard Wagners und ihrer Quellen*, Mainz 1986, p. 159). He advertised the occasion with an announcement in the *Neue freie Presse*, describing *Norma* as 'of all Bellini's creations . . . the richest in the profoundly realistic way in which true melody is united with intimate passion' (translated from Tintori 1983, p. 176).

A few days before the performance he issued a further piece of advance publicity in the *Rigaer Zuschauer* in the form of the essay 'Bellini: a word in season,' from which the following is taken.

Bellinian music, that is to say Bellinian song, has recently attracted such attention, even in deeply learned Germany, and has inflamed such enthusiasm, that simply as a phenomenon in its own right it would be well worth investigating. That Bellinian song should delight in Italy and France is simple and natural – for in Italy and France one listens with one's ears, hence such phrases of ours as 'ear-tickling' and so on – (presumably in contrast to the 'eye-itching' which . . . is caused us in the reading of so many scores of more recent German operas) – but that even the German musical connoisseur removed his spectacles from his weary eyes and for once surrendered recklessly to the joy of beautiful song, that at once allows us to peer deeper into his real heart. And there one perceives a profound and ardent yearning to breathe freely and deeply, to make things at a stroke simpler for oneself and throw away all the pomposity of prejudice and pedantry, which for so long forced one to be a German musical connoisseur, and instead of that at last to be a human being for once, happy, free, and endowed with all the splendid organs of receptivity for everything beautiful, let it manifest itself in whatever form it will.

Because how little convinced we really are by all the nonsensical junk of prejudice and presumption. How often may it have happened to us that we have been enchanted in listening to an Italian or French opera; but when we left the theatre we laughed off our excitement with a pitying witticism, and then, when we reached home, we persuaded ourselves that one really must guard against enthusiasm. But if, for once, we don't make this witticism and don't persuade ourselves in this way, and if instead we hold fast to that which has just delighted us, then we shall learn, particularly in the case of Bellini, that it was pure melody, noble and beautiful song, that enchanted us. To cherish this and to believe in it is surely no sin: it is perhaps not even a sin if, before going to sleep, one sends a prayer heavenwards that such melodies and such a way of treating song might for once occur to German composers.

Song, song, and once again song, ye Germans! For in fact song is the language in which man should express himself musically, and if it is not independently cultivated and preserved, as every other educated language should be, then you will not be understood. For the rest, what is bad in this man Bellini could certainly be better done by any of your German village schoolmasters; that is well-known. So it is quite beside the point to make fun of these shortcomings. Had Bellini studied with a German village schoolmaster he would probably have learned to do things better. It is, however, much to be feared that he might at the same time have unlearned his art of song . . .

The form and style of the Italians is, in its decadence, certainly one-dimensional and over-flowery. But in his *Norma*, indisputably his most successful composition, Bellini provides a demonstration of how serviceable this style can be, particularly with some operatic subjects. Here, where even the poetry raises itself to the tragic heights of the ancient Greeks, this sense of form, which Bellini most decidedly ennobles, serves only to heighten the solemn and grandiose character of the whole. All the passions, transfigured in so singular a fashion by his song, derive therefrom a majestic solidity and well-foundedness. And on this foundation they do not flutter about vaguely, but form themselves into a grand and clear picture which involuntarily reminds us of the creations of Gluck and Spontini. (Wagner 1983b, pp. 25–7)

Schumann and Liszt

Schumann at first, in the *Damenkonversationslexikon* of 1834, for example, wrote encouragingly rather than enthusiastically about Bellini, envisaging him by 'a serious study of German music' being enabled to 'put an end to the shallow, effeminate musical style of the newer Italian school'. His later disillusion may in part have been due to the depressing regularity with which virtuoso fantasias and variation sets on Italian operatic themes fell on his editorial desk. I do not propose to describe those by Diabelli, Hünten, Louise Farrenc, Bottesini (for double-bass) or Thalberg, though Thalberg's *Norma* fantasia (Op. 12) was interesting enough to have been in the repertory of both Brahms and Mahler in their school-days.

One of these virtuoso fantasias does however merit closer attention. Liszt's 'Réminiscences de Norma' is a rare example of this, in principle fascinating, in practice so often depressing genre, that perhaps merits the description masterpiece. (Deathridge (1988, p. 225) regards it as 'a piece of transcendental humbug'.) At very least it is remarkable as a piece of creative criticism. The 'Réminiscences' were composed in 1843 (according to the Peters edition) or 1844 (*New Grove*) with a dedication to Camille Pleyel, Berlioz's Camille Moke, dedicatee also of his 'Tarantelle di Bravura' based on Auber's *La muette de Portici* and of Chopin's Op. 9 Nocturnes. In 1874 Liszt issued an arrangement for two pianos.

Unlike his *Lucia di Lammermoor* 'reminiscences', which are essentially a transcription of the great sextet, or the *Don Giovanni* 'reminiscences', in which the Commendatore's intimations of doom frame bravura variations on two of Mozart's most apparently artless numbers ('Là ci darem' and 'Fin ch'han dal vino'), the 'reminiscences' of *Norma* range relatively widely over the opera, laying particular emphasis on its opening and closing scenes. Liszt designs his work in three linked movements in mediantly related keys: (i) an Introduction and first movement in G, based on the music of the Gaulish priests and warriors; (ii) a slow movement in B based on the Act II finale; (iii) what one might describe as a march-scherzo leading into a finale-apotheosis, all in E♭, based respectively on the *Coro di guerra* and the finale again. In Appendix 3 I have provided a fuller account of Liszt's piece; here it will be sufficient simply to enumerate the critical points that are suggested by the 'Réminiscences' – that the central tragic theme is that of the vulnerable individual engulfed and destroyed by political, religious and social circumstance, yet ultimately transcending it; that a fantastic exertion of Liszt's virtuosic imagination is needed to match the sheer intoxicating sensuousness of Bellini's music; that over and over again the music possesses a quality of lulling, repetitive circularity which offers much scope to the fancy of the virtuoso performer (whether transcriber-pianist or, by implication, singer); that much of the music is pervaded by common thematic or rhythmic elements; that the quiddity of some of Bellini's apparently cruder passages is a positive to be savoured rather than an embarrassment to be hidden; that anyone with a sophisticated harmonic imagination is sorely tempted to enrich Bellini's harmonic vocabulary; that Italian *bel canto* transcribes so gorgeously for the piano, that it is readily and unsurprisingly perceivable as one of the primary sources for Liszt's and for Chopin's musical language.

Giuseppe Rovani

By the middle decades of the century, back in Italy, *Norma* had come to be seen as the representative masterpiece of its age. We may allow the novelist Giuseppe Rovani (1818–74), writing in 1858, in the last years before the emergence of Italy as a nation-state, to evoke for us what the opera meant to Italian opera-lovers of his generation.

On almost every occasion when we have been present at a revival of NORMA, whether in Milan or elsewhere, whether in large theatres or in small, we have always observed the same phenomena: a kind of contentment in the public before the curtain rises; something like a ray of youth returning to the brows of the old habitués of the theatre as they listen once more to those sublime conceptions; an unusual attentiveness in the young people, who learned that music from tradition, and a hint of an inclination on their part to break faith with the modern idols; and after all this – such is the sway of the music – a critical indulgence towards the performers, who, if they are good are treated as outstanding, if they are mediocre are received as if they were good, and if someone among them is in danger of not even rising to mediocrity, the good humour is such that no-one wants to spoil the family festival for a nonentity.

And all these things happened again on the first evening of the staging of this new NORMA. So we find ourselves obliged to repeat that with this opera Bellini has furnished an insuperable model of lyric tragedy, a model so lofty that it may be accorded the status of the ideal (il quale può assurgere fino al rango del ideale) . . . This work holds in safekeeping all those laws of art which are not arbitrary but stand firm upon truth, upon feeling and upon the mysterious agreement of taste with the sway of absolute beauty. (Quoted in Branca 1882, pp. 174–5)

8 *Critical fortunes since the Unification of Italy*

It was typical of the young Richard Wagner that he did not merely enthuse about *Norma*: he reflected on it philosophically and found a way of placing it in a framework created by his own vision of operatic history. As the years passed, as the world in which Bellini had lived and worked was superseded by a very different world, in which Italy had become a free and united nation, and in which the opera-houses of the peninsula were exploring a more cosmopolitan repertory, Italian reactions to *Norma* also became more thoughtful.

We may remain for a moment with Giuseppe Rovani who, by the 1860s, had become the unofficial leader of the group of Milanese artists and intellectuals known as the 'scapigliati' – the 'dishevelled ones'. As a novelist Rovani was a relatively old-fashioned figure; so he was as a musical connoisseur. But as a theorist of the arts he opened the eyes of his younger contemporaries to exciting new vistas, particularly by insisting upon those Baudelairean *correspondances* that mysteriously linked the various arts together.

In his most substantial aesthetic writing, *Le tre arti* of 1874, Bellini holds a place of honour. The first two paragraphs of the following excerpt are from the preface, in which Rovani explains his historical and philosophical presuppositions; the remainder is from the body of the book, the chapter entitled simply 'Vincenzo Bellini'. Rovani's reflections on *Norma* are those of a patriot who had lived through the heroic decades of the *risorgimento*, and of a lover of traditional opera, who had experienced, and did not care for, the first stirrings of 'music drama'.

In following the history of thought and of the forward march of civilization it is of the greatest interest to observe the simultaneous progress of the three sister arts – of words, of images, of tones – which, like the Graces, always remain bound indissolubly together. Everywhere where civilization has penetrated and where it continues its course, we see the phases of thought unfold in a threefold manifestation. Poetry, nourished by the meditation of the philosophers and prepared by the events of history, is first to find the concept and, clothed in forms now sublime, now graceful, but almost always inaccessible to the multitude, would tend the flame only for the rarest spirits of humanity, were it not that music, by way of the senses, conveys the discoveries of poetry to all mortals; they, whether they will or no, learn from music to become agitated, to be angry, to be comforted, or to rise to a pitch of enthusiasm. But the waves of music are too fugitive, and the impressions derived from them are cancelled out one by the other [. . . and would] fade away in a white mist, were it not that sculpture and painting, with their solid physicality (segni fissi) give tangible form to the idea that springs from poetry, and transform it into visible shapes. [Rovani goes on to explain that this advance of the three arts in fellowship has continued longest and is seen most clearly in Italy.]

To the fecund and . . . epicurean inspiration of the previous age succeeded an austere and sober inspiration . . . Grossi's *Ildegonda* drew tears from every beautiful eye in the peninsula, and from that day on it seemed barely decent, rather uncivilized, to abandon oneself to the unseemly exertions of mirth . . . Even the lively colours that blossom on healthy and happy young faces fell completely in price, while instead pale cheeks and languishing eyes acquired an inestimable value. [With this general enthusiasm for weeping, *opera buffa* went out of fashion completely.] And behold, from the southernmost extreme of Italy, as if expressly to prove the general concord, the Master of Catania responded to the invitations of the Lombard poets with the most melodious of sighs. And then, from the sphere of solitary thinkers and of those sentimental fair ones who read unwearyingly, armed with their tear-drenched handkerchiefs, sadness descended to the ordinary people who, in the 'furor delle tempeste' and the 'stragi' of *Il pirata* learned to forget the 'Largo al factotum della città' which in earlier times . . . had enlivened the nocturnal silence of the public streets. And the plastic arts, anxious to be received appreciatively by the multitude for whom they are intended, did not delay in associating themselves with poetry and music. So then, in the kiss of *Romeo and Juliet*, and in the death of *Clorinda*, and on the scaffold of *Mary Stuart*, and above all in the general style of those paintings, one saw that Grossi, embraced by Bellini, had passed the word of command to Hayez.

For anyone who would say that Bellini distinguished himself only in the expression of intimate emotions, like Virgil, we reply that in *Norma*, while he retains his place within the sweet dominion of feeling, he also emerges from it to occupy regions more arduous and more vast. Here it is not simply a matter of domestic passions developed with sovereign mastery, but two nations are set face to face in a twofold manifestation of the very nature of their being; here are rendered the aspirations of the multitude; here two religious creeds are placed in conflict; here, in the person of Pollione, is represented the voluptuous grandeur of Rome in its period of decadence, and the distant announcement of the barbarian domination; here, in the bardic songs of the warriors of Irminsul, and in the naive sighs of Adalgisa, and in the sublime wrath of Norma, and in the pagan love of the pro-consul, are arrayed all the elements through which modern drama loves to overwhelm us (sono percorsi tutti gli elementi onde ama di essere dominatrice la drammatica moderna).

The Bellinian structure was brought to perfection in *Norma*; indeed we are disposed to say that, in this wonderul work, dramatic-lyrical music [i.e. opera] has embraced the full scope which reason, creative fantasy and good taste allow it; if it trespass beyond this, music is led into ways false to its own nature, and . . . is led to forfeit, either in whole or in part, its own proper strengths in the dishonest attempt to acquire attributes to which it has no claim. The lyric drama which forces itself to compete with spoken drama bastardizes the music, while it inhibits the independent and free development of the spoken drama; thus there results from the adulterated and incomplete contributions of the two arts a hybrid art which, like Corinthian brass, is neither gold nor silver, neither wood nor steel, but an artificial mishmash.

Bellini's principal merit, which after all is the supreme virtue governing works of the mind as it is the supreme virtue governing moral behaviour, is an unshakeable loyalty to his own principles; it is a love of art religious and devout enough to silence the love of self and of fleeting applause; it is that unalterable calm of mind which knows how to conjoin all the ideas and forms of art in a powerful unity which never fails.

From the far end of Italy at about the same time came another noteworthy assessment of Bellini's historical and aesthetic significance. Antonio Tari was Professor of Aesthetics at the University of Naples from 1861 to his death in 1884, a period which, despite Unification in 1861 and the consequent loss of its status as a capital, Naples had certainly not yet lost its standing as one of the two or three most intellectually vital cities in Italy. The essay 'Vincenzo Bellini' first appeared in 1876. In 1911 it was reissued in a collection of Tari's writings edited by Benedetto Croce, with an *Avvertenza* which gives due warning of the eccentricity of Tari's style. Croce confesses that

until a few years ago I should have lacked the courage to lay this volume before the Italian public. But now that, on the one hand, a certain interest in speculative studies has reawakened and, on the other, literary taste has become broader and is no longer resistant to or repelled by styles of exposition that are fantastic, capricious and humorous, I entertain the hope that these essays . . . will not be judged, as they inevitably would have been a few years ago, obscure and horribly written, and that they will indeed find a curious, attentive and intelligent readership.

(Tari's) personality, trembling with sympathetic emotion when faced with works of art, overflowing with enthusiasm, gifted with a benevolence and nobility of feeling which always remained fresh and pure like that of a child, inspired him to write pages which are of a kind very rare in our literature, and which could only have arisen from a mind cultivated in German romantic literature, but which, for all its culture and predilections, did not lose the qualities of the southerner, clear-sighted and slightly teasing.

Despite Croce's apology, a very small sample of Tari's Bellini essay is likely to suffice for the modern reader.

Here [in *Norma*] is something I call a genuine triumph, a spectacle at which any thoughtful critic must raise his eyebrows. Here the Tragic is triumphantly lyricized, and the cothurnus of sesquipedalian polyphony is outrun by the light sandal of winged song. O you theatrical swindlers, o you forgers not even of gold coinage, but of the vile paper currency of superficial effects, which you call Drama, of noise, which you take for Passion, of the enigmatic, which you suppose to be Character; you who cannot have too much of trumpets and drums and cannons to torment the audience's ears; if you are passing by, stop and tell me; can there be any sorrow like unto the sorrow of Norma?

(In the incomparable 'In mia man alfin tu sei') notice the complete interpenetration of text and music, which here seem not to have been generated in the brains of two distinct personalities, poet and musician, Felice Romani and Bellini, but to have materialized in a unique, double-formed organism, where consequently the music seems the effect of the poetry, and the poetry the effect of the music (e quindi musicati in quanto poetati, e poetati in quanto musicati). This is such a singular case of interpenetration that it strikes the listener with the force of an electric shock, filling him with awe (raccapriccio), like any lightning flash of the divine striking to earth. . . .

At times Bellini subordinated the accompaniment to the song, at times he co-ordinated them, but never did the accompaniment predominate. The effects that can be achieved through tones (le efficienze tonali) are that which they are, that is to say, the vehicles of musical *pathos* and nothing more. On whichever *pathos* holds the hegemony depends the choice of arms; and [musical] Technique, like some skilled pancratist, will here gain the victory by wrestling naked, and will there succeed in conquering difficulties by striking with trumpets and drums, like a pugilist . . .

It is worth remembering the saying of those critics who, in comparing the Parthenon with a Gothic cathedral, have judged that the former, stripped as it is of its polychrome and its other architectural adornments, could be likened to a beautiful naked girl; whereas the cathedral, without its trimmings of stone tracery-work, would appear to the spectator like the skeleton of an old woman, whose ribbons and nick-nacks only serve to falsify and distort her form. Say the same, gentle reader, of Bellinian polyphony compared with many scores of Wagnerizing composers, and you will hit the target.

Indeed, *macte animo*, and I shall affirm something that: will seem very strange. And that is, that Bellini should be regarded as an embryonic Wagner: that same Bellini who, in his own generation, wanted and attempted the same operatic renewal that Gluck initiated and which, as the third like-minded person (terzo tra cotanto senno), the German innovator has not yet succeeded in solemnizing in his wondrous baptistery at Bayreuth. . . .

I think I can assert without fear of misunderstanding that: either there will be no musical palingenesis in the future; or that, even if there is, it will certainly not enfeeble melody by turning it into melopoeia, will not freeze recitative into declamation, and above all will not dissolve those precious pearls . . . which are called themes in an acid solution of continuously endless phraseology without phrases.

So Bellinism, developed, amplified, but always given lyric form by other Italian Orpheuses of Bellinian stock, will very probably some day become the true and longed-for MUSIC OF THE FUTURE.

In the meantime, what were the musicians making of Bellini? For, clearly, it was hardly possible, in an age increasingly pervaded by Wagnerian aesthetics, and when even Italian opera-goers were becoming increasingly familiar with Meyerbeer, Bizet and Massenet, to respond to Bellini's music with the naive raptures of the 1830s. The reputation of *Norma*, however, remained astonishingly high, and not only in Italy. During the protracted artistic crisis that blighted Bizet's middle years in the 1860s – when he was trying to persuade himself that, though he 'sometimes got lost in artistic houses of ill-fame', for he 'loved Italian music as one loves a courtesan', he was really 'German by conviction, heart and soul' – 'two-thirds' of *Norma* nevertheless seemed not only lovable but admirable, a higher proportion than of any other Italian opera he names in a famous letter written in March 1867.[1] Brahms was happy to endorse Hermann Levi's view that 'in Bellini's *Norma* there are really quite extraordinary and beautiful things' (Deathridge 1988, p. 227). So he will have been gratified as well as amused to learn from Hans von Bülow that Kaiser Wilhelm I, whose favourite composer Bellini was, regarded as 'a second Bellini — Brahms!' (Bülow, *Briefe* 1886). Mahler, who, like Brahms, made one of his first public appearances as a pianist playing Thalberg's *Norma* fantasy, was also an admirer. He conducted the opera in Hamburg in 1896 with Anna Mildenburg in the leading role. Despite confessing that it was 'difficult and strange' for a conductor of his type simply to accompany the singers, he confessed to Natalie Bauer-Lechner, whom he invited to one of the performances, that some passages moved him to tears: 'how I should like to hear *Norma* for the first time, and hear it conducted by myself! I envy you' (de La Grange 1973, p. 348).

The views of one composer are especially interesting and have become particularly influential.

In the summer of 1832, a few months after the first run of *Norma* performances had finished, the young Verdi arrived in Milan to commence his musical studies there. When, at the insistence of his teacher

Vincenzo Lavigna, he acquired a season ticket for La Scala, the repertory he would have heard in the period from 1832 to June 1834, and again from January to the summer of 1835 included a number of revivals of the opera, some with Pasta in the principal role, others with Malibran (Tintori, *Cronologia*, in Gatti 1964).

These performances must be supposed to have impressed him deeply: Bellini is one of the most important sources of his own style. However, as far as the surviving evidence shows, many years were to pass before Verdi expressed any clearly articulated opinion of the older composer's work. His feelings about Bellini seem to have come into focus (or into the open) in 1871, at a time when he was giving much thought to questions of musical education. To Giuseppe Piroli, a friend and local member of parliament who was picking his brains about the teaching in Italian conservatories, Verdi remarked in passing, 'Bellini possessed exceptional qualities such as no Conservatory can impart and lacked those which a Conservatory ought to have taught him' (letter of 7 February 1871, *Carteggi verdiani III*, ed. A. Luzio, Rome 1947, p. 79, translated Budden 1981, p. 266).

That view may be said to have remained constant for the last thirty years of Verdi's life, though it might be subtly shaded or re-emphasized depending on the context in which he is speaking, and the detail might be filled out a little. Overwhelmingly, that context was provided by Verdi's sense that Italian music was in danger of losing its way, that Italian composers, made nervous and self-conscious by a new breed of over-clever, cosmopolitan and 'progressive' music critics, were betraying or falsifying their national traditions. Under these circumstances Bellini, in both his strengths and in what Verdi believed to be his weaknesses, became something of an emblematic figure, a symbol of beleaguered *italianità*. I quote excerpts from three of Verdi's letters:

(i) from a letter written from Naples to Clarina Maffei, 9 April 1873
[Aida had been well received in Naples, remarks Verdi, enjoyed spontaneously and enthusiastically.] And do you know why? Because there are no critics here, behaving like the apostles; nor the swarms of *maestri* who know nothing about music except what they have studied according to the models of Mendelssohn, Schumann, Wagner, etc.; nor the aristocratic dilettantism with its modish raptures for everything it doesn't understand. And what is the result of all that? Error and confusion in the heads of the young.

Let me explain. Just imagine what would happen today to a young man of the type of Bellini, not very self-confident, indecisive because of his limited studies, simply led by his instincts; then used as a butt for the criticism of Filippi and the Wagnerians, etc. He would finish up with absolutely no self-confidence left, and perhaps be lost . . . Amen, Amen. (F. Abbiati, *Verdi*, Milan 1959, vol. III, pp. 631–2)

(ii) from a letter written from Genoa to Giulio Ricordi, 20 November 1880
[The topic in hand is the revision of *Simon Boccanegra* that Verdi was making in collaboration with Boito. This task involved a confronting of the musical styles of the 1850s from the perspective of 1880, an experience that occasionally prompted Verdi to air his views on matters aesthetic and philosophical. Bellini, invoked only indirectly through the names of some of his arias, is here posited as the wholesome antidote – simple, natural, spontaneous – to many of the problems of contemporary opera. Verdi remarks that the revision of *Simon Boccanegra* might entail the retention of some of the original cabalettas.] *Open, o earth!* I don't have such a horror of cabalettas, though, and if tomorrow a youngster should be born who could write me one as fine as 'Meco tu vieni o misera', for instance, or 'Ah, perchè non posso odiarti', I'd be absolutely delighted to hear them, and I would renounce all the harmonic quibbles, all the affectations of our learned orchestrations . . . Ah, progress, science, realism . . .. alas, alas [. . .] The irony is that with all this progress art turns backwards. Art lacking spontaneity, naturalness and simplicity is no longer art. (*Carteggio Verdi – Ricordi 1880–1881*, ed. P. Petrobelli, Parma 1988, p. 70)

(iii) from a letter written to Camille Bellaigue, 2 May 1898
[Bellaigue had sent Verdi a copy of his recently published *Portraits et silhouettes de musiciens*, which includes a study of Bellini. In acknowledging the book Verdi counters some of Bellaigue's remarks about Italian composers and, in particular, is moved to make the most complete avowal of his feelings for Bellini. These few sentences are so telling that they have remained the fundamental perceptions of Bellini criticism down to our own time.] It's true that Bellini is poor in harmony and orchestration! . . . but rich in feeling and in a melancholy entirely his own. Even in his less-known operas, in *Straniera* and *Pirata*, there are long, long melodies such as no one wrote before him. And how much truth and power of declamation there is especially in the duet between Pollione and Norma! And how much loftiness of thought in the first phrase of the Introduzione of *Norma*, followed after a few bars by another phrase [here he quotes two bars of it: the passage beginning one bar after Fig. 10] which is badly scored but which no one has surpassed for heavenly beauty. (*Copialettere*, ed. G. Cesari & A. Luzio, Milan 1913, p. 416, translated Budden 1981, p. 152)

Brahms and Mahler probably, Verdi very certainly, are in their various ways all expressing the predominant view of the half-century that extended from the 1860s to the First World War. The beauties of Bellini's art are unmistakable and irresistible; if they move and enthral us only spasmodically it is, in part, because these beauties are embedded in a dramatic framework the aesthetic validity of which has been undermined by the philosophy of the music drama; in part because, in a musical world in which harmonic and orchestral sophistication have become everyday events, Bellini's musical language often seems one-dimensional. The same point of view is expounded in the writings of Eduard Hanslick and Ferdinand Hiller, both warm admirers, and might be said to come to its picturesque climax in Cecil Gray's Sicilian metaphors; in the case of *Norma*, Gray evokes images of 'the ruined temples of Girgenti [Agrigento], a few lovely columns standing up proudly from a mound of rubble, facing Africa' (*Contingencies*, London 1947, p. 118).

Earlier in this essay Gray had remarked that, at the time of writing (1922), it had long been the established view that 'Bellini, together with his companion in crime, Donizetti, represents the nadir of music' (*ibid.*, p. 105). Even allowing for the fact that Gray never believed in understating his case, he is not quite up-to-date here. For some years before he wrote, Bellini had in fact become an object of intense interest to the *generazione dell'ottanta*. Both the most ebullient controversialist of the 'generation', Fausto Torrefranca, and the group's most conservative and high-minded composer, Ildebrando Pizzetti, wrote extensively about him. To be sure, this was in part because they felt that Bellini served as a useful stick with which to beat the sensational cosmopolitanism of Puccini. Pizzetti's essays are particularly noteworthy for his attempt to get beyond the condescending view that Bellini's music is good in part, or good considering that he had to work in a discredited tradition; if this is great art, it behoves us to approach it and try to understand it on its own terms. Pizzetti explores with particular care Bellini's relationship with Romani, and expounds the concept of what he calls 'pure song'. The following excerpts are from the long essay 'La musica di Vincenzo Bellini', written in 1915.

[The importance to Bellini of Romani was not that he was particularly original, or had a different concept of the melodrama.] But a different kind of poetry, yes, that was something he could give him . . . Creator of forms of perfect purity and sovereign elegance, Bellini must necessarily have detested the slovenly, fatuously verbose poetry of a Tottola or a Giraldoni, and could not but love (Romani's) beautifully harmonious verses, the tastefully chosen imagery, bold without rashness, neither commonplace nor yet eccentric, its words wisely employed, with a sense of their power, their importance and their effect . . . But to recognize a resemblance and affinity in their aesthetic sense is far from claiming that Romani's poetry decisively influenced the direction and the development of Bellini's art. [If Bellini had lived longer, he might, like Verdi, have outlived his dependence upon librettists. But while Verdi recognized a spiritual brother in Shakespeare] Bellini, a lyrico-dramatic genius, but incomparably more lyrical than dramatic, would perhaps have finished by going back to Greek tragedy. One need only think what the final scenes of *Iphigenia* might have become, set to music by him, to deplore in his death the loss of some divine miracle of musical beauty.

[Pizzetti examines *Il pirata* to show that there can be no doubt that, in terms of form, counterpoint, etc., Bellini had fully mastered his *métier*.] (However,) it is easy to understand that Bellini must have felt, for his own part, the uselessness of the contrapuntal forms. He was a pure lyricist . . . a creator who must have felt art not as an expression of conflicts, of life in a state of continuous becoming, but as a resolution of drama, as a purification of emotional travails. He must therefore have felt that, for him, there could be only one true form of expression, or at any rate that one form of expression had to predominate: the linear form of pure song. And while this song might well gain lights and shadows from the accompaniment, with its mysterious generative harmonies, might indeed be intensified and have its expressive power thrown into relief by them, nevertheless it would have to bear every essential element of its beauty in itself, in its shape, its movement and its accents.

[Pizzetti discusses this concept of 'pure song' at some length.] In purely instrumental music, the beauty of a design [disegno] in sound or of an arabesque in sound resides above all in the very lines of the design, in the hieroglyphics of the arabesque. It is a beauty which, so to speak, is seen; the beauty of song, of pure song, of truly vocal song, resides in its spirit and in its very motivating force [nel perchè della cosa], and is a beauty which is experienced . . . We shall find that, whereas music that is pure sonorous play, lacking the quality of vocalism . . . depends for its aesthetic effect on the more or less rich and admirable and interesting architectonic structure, music which exists as the pure expression of emotion, as pure song . . . is asymmetrical, irregular, anti-architectonic, and we shall find it that much more irregular and anti-architectonic (that is, that much the more expansive from pure interior necessity) wherever it has most moved us . . . Bellini's most beautiful arias are precisely the most anti-architectonic, those with the freest strophic structure, or indeed with no such structure at all, those without reprises and repetitions . . . And since the character of song, of *vocalità*, is independent of the architectonic extension and construction of the musical expression, one may very well find more song in a fragment of recitative than in a long aria of a hundred bars.

. . . We can very well say that emotion cannot be found except in song, cannot be expressed musically except with the character of *vocalità*; in fact it can be only song, pure and naked line, isolated even from its own generating harmonies. Music felt as the linear and virtually naked expression of emotion, Bellini felt to be his own most personal and natural kind of musical expression, and it is this that I have aimed to define in the words pure song.

[Pizzetti analyses 'Dormono entrambi' and the recitative of the following duet, which he admires far less. He remarks that when one comes across a Bellinian aria that, for all its charm, fails to move us deeply, almost always it will be found to be a piece without any real dependence upon the poetry.] When Bellini said, 'Give me good poetry and I will give you good music', he said something very apt, in that he recognized that the greater or lesser expressive profundity and aesthetic perfection of his music would always be at the rate of the object which had inspired it, that is to say that his music will have sprung from deeper springs, and will have soared to loftier heights, depending upon the profundity and power of the emotions that generated it. [Compared with the situation in Rossini] in a Bellini opera one can be certain *a priori*, that no great beauties will be found, no profound and essential beauties, except in those arias that have been experienced as the expression of the most important moments of the whole opera from the point of view of feeling and of representation. [After a very full discussion of the Act II finale, Pizzetti draws this part of his argument to a close as follows:] Bellini's lyricism – can we say that this has now been sufficiently demonstrated? – is not only always born as the expressive resolution and conclusion of the drama; it is also the sublimation (*superamento*) of the drama. It is a kind of song which pours out as the essential expression of an emotion aroused by the drama, especially in the drama's points of resolution, just as a fire flares up where the rays of a warm light are made to converge. And it is a kind of song that, hardly has it begun to flow than it becomes a stream, and soon it has become a river, and then an ocean, the waves of which roll away to the vast horizon in the distance.

Since World War II academic musicology has begun to come to terms with Bellini. In a notable series of essays Friedrich Lippmann has subjected Bellini's music to the same kinds of scrutiny as had long been customary with the German and French repertories, analysing the ingredients of his musical language, its formal qualities, the interdependence of poetic and musical structures and so on. Simon Maguire's 1989 study, *Vincenzo Bellini and the aesthetics of early nineteenth-century Italian opera*, valuably complements Lippmann by setting the operas back in the kind of aesthetic framework within which they were first conceived. It has not been part of Lippmann's or Maguire's purpose to investigate the qualities that make *Norma*, or any other Bellini opera, an individual, unique masterpiece. Of the critical essays that *have* made such an investigation those by Erasmi and Joly, the one predominantly socio-political in orientation, the other psychological, are particularly valuable.

9 *Five prima donnas: contributions to a performance history*

In any performance in Bellini's masterpiece, Norma's is the role that counts. Pollione ranks with Pinkerton among the most graceless tenors in the repertory; Adalgisa, whose exquisitely tender and passionate role was downgraded by Bellini in a seemingly definitive revision of the opera soon after its first publication, disappears entirely from the scene as the drama approaches its climax; and Oroveso's part is less imposingly monumental than it might have been, for Bellini trimmed it out of consideration for an artist in fragile health. None of this is to imply that these roles do not need musical and imaginative singing. But no other full-length opera in the repertory depends so heavily and mercilessly for its success on the prima donna.

Bellini composed *Norma* for Giuditta Pasta, the woman he once called an 'encyclopaedic angel' (letter of 28 April 1832). And that meant that the role was calculated to explore and challenge the voice, and to extend to its very limits the art, of the greatest singer of the age. The role has come to be seen as 'the very acme of the soprano's repertory . . . more challenging than Brünnhilde or Isolde' (Christiansen 1984, p. 66), 'ten times as exacting as Leonore' in Lilli Lehmann's judgement (Porter 1979, p. 154). Toscanini, who shared the widely-held conviction that *Norma* was the masterpiece of the *bel canto* repertory, never performed the opera because, in Tullio Serafin's view, 'he never found a soprano who could adequately realize the protagonist he had in mind' (quoted in G. R. Marek, *Toscanini*, New York 1975, p. 63). Herbert von Karajan, though he believed he had found the perfect Adalgisa in Agnes Baltsa, never recorded it, apparently for similar reasons (Matheopoulos 1992, p. 240).

I propose therefore to make this chapter simply a tale of five prima donnas.

Giuditta Pasta (1797–1865)

The first must clearly be Bellini's own Norma. Pasta's reputation was earned in the music of an earlier generation: in Mozart, Cimarosa, Paisiello, Zingarelli. As she approached her prime, the operas of Rossini provided her with several of her greatest roles, and it is in Stendhal's biography of Rossini that we find the most eloquent tributes to her art. That incomparable compendium of extravagant enthusiams reaches one of its climaxes in its long thirty-fifth chapter, entitled 'Madame Pasta', from which the following excerpts are taken:

. . . an actress who is young and beautiful; who is both intelligent and sensitive; whose gestures never deteriorate from the plainest and most natural modes of simplicity, and yet manage to keep faith with the purest ideals of formal beauty . . . a voice which can weave a spell of magic about the plainest word in the plainest recitative; a voice whose compelling inflexions can subdue the most recalcitrant and obdurate hearts, and oblige them to share in the emotions which radiate from some great aria. (Stendhal, *The Life of Rossini*, translated and edited by Richard N. Coe, New York and London 1985, pp. 371–2)

Madame Pasta's voice has a considerable range. She can achieve perfect resonance on a note as low as bottom A, and can rise as high as C♯, or even to a slightly sharpened D; and she possesses the rare ability to be able to sing contralto as easily as she can sing soprano. I would suggest . . . that the true designation of her voice is *mezzo-soprano*, and any composer who writes for her should use the *mezzo-soprano* range for the thematic material of his music, while still exploiting, as it were incidentally and from time to time, notes which lie within the more peripheral areas of this remarkably rich voice. Many notes of this last category are not only extremely fine in themselves, but have the ability to produce a kind of resonant and magnetic vibration, which, through some still unexplained combination of physical phenomena, exercises an instantaneous and hypnotic effect upon the soul of the spectator.

This leads me to the consideration of one of the most uncommon features of Madame Pasta's voice: it is *not all moulded from the same metallo*, as they would say in Italy (i.e. it possesses more then one *timbre*); and this fundamental variety of tone produced by a single voice affords one of the richest veins of musical expression which the artistry of a great *cantatrice* is able to exploit. (*Ibid.*, p. 374)

Madame Pasta's incredible mastery of technique is revealed in the amazing facility with which she alternates head-notes with chest-notes; she possesses to a superlative degree the art of producing an immense variety of charming and thrilling effects from the use of *both* voices. To heighten the tonal colouring of a melodic phrase, or to pass in a flash from one *ambiance* to another infinitely removed from it, she is accustomed to use a *falsetto* technique covering notes right down to the middle of her normal range; or else she may unconcernedly alternate *falsetto* notes with ordinary chest-notes . . .

Extremely reserved in her use of *fioriture*, she resorts to them *only* when they have a direct contribution to make to the dramatic expressiveness of the music; and it is worth noting that none of her *fioriture* are retained for a single instant after they have ceased to be useful . . .[1] (*Ibid.*, p. 378)

Pasta's art ripened as a new, more romantic and passionate style of music took possession of the Italian opera-house, and she created roles for Pacini and Donizetti (including Anna Bolena) as well as for Bellini. *Norma*, in which she made her La Scala debut in 1831, marked the summit of her career. Everything we know about the circumstances of its composition suggests that it was tailored to her particular qualities as a singer and musician; no singer ever earned a nobler monument.

While tributes to Pasta's art comparable to Stendhal's are to be found in many contemporary writings, most critics go on to make a further point: that Pasta was not an effortless or easy singer; that her accomplishments were a triumph of intelligence, musicianship and will over what were, in their state of nature, very imperfect endowments. In Chorley's words, 'No candidate for musical sovereignty ever presented herself with what must have seemed a more slender and imperfect list of credentials' (Chorley 1862, vol. I, p. 128). And he continues:

she subjected herself to a course of severe and incessant vocal study, to subdue and utilize her voice. To equalize it was impossible. There was a portion of the scale which differed from the rest in quality, and remained to the last 'under a veil', to use the Italian term. There were notes always more or less out of tune,[2] especially at the commencement of her performance. Out of these uncouth materials she had to compose her instrument, and then to give it flexibility. Her studies to acquire execution must have been tremendous; but the volubility and brilliance, when acquired, gained a character of their own, from the resisting peculiarities of the organ. There were a breadth, an expressiveness in her *roulades*, an evenness and solidity in her shake, which imparted to every passage a significance totally beyond the reach of lighter and more spontaneous singers.[3] (*Ibid.*, p. 129)

Sadly Chorley left no account of Pasta's Norma, beyond remarking that, when he heard her in the role in London, 'the glory of [her] voice already showed signs of waning: she steadily began her evening's task half a tone too flat. Her acting was more powerful and striking than

5. 'Giuditta Pasta in the role of Norma', portrait by François Gérard, between 1831 and 1835.

ever, if that could be' (*ibid.*, p. 61). (There is, however, a wonderful account of her in Mayr's *Medea in Corinto* (*ibid.*, pp. 133–4).)

In the Act I finale, it was apparently Pasta who 'after the first performance, speeded up ("Oh! di qual sei tu vittima"), as it is sung today [1882], giving it an elan which the composer himself had not imagined. Subsequently the opportunity was taken to cut one of the repeats, and the stretta too was performed just once' (D'Arcais 1882, p. 811).

Giulia Grisi (1811–1869)

The Adalgisa who sang alongside Pasta at the Milan premiere of *Norma*, Giulia Grisi, was to create almost as indelible a mark on her contemporaries. Her career was to be based largely in Paris and London, and there she came to be regarded as the supreme Bellinian soprano of the middle decades of the century. As one of the 'Puritani quartet' based at the Théâtre Italien in 1835, Grisi is most commonly associated with the limper and more pathetic heroine of Bellini's last opera. Clearly she was a very different kind of singer from Pasta. Chorley describes her thus:

> what a *soprano* voice was hers! – rich, sweet – equal throughout its compass of two octaves (from C to C) without a break, or a note which had to be managed . . . Her shake was clear and rapid; her scales were certain; every interval was taken without hesitation by her. Nor has any woman ever more thoroughly commanded every gradation of force than she . . . the clear, penetrating beauty of her reduced tones . . . was so unique, as to reconcile the ear to a certain shallowness of expression in her rendering of the words and the situation. (Chorley 1862, vol. I, pp. 110–11)

It was no doubt this last limitation that made Bellini sceptical of her ability to sustain such a role as Norma.

> Give her *La Sonnambula*, or *Puritani* or *La gazza [ladra]*, and a thousand operas of simple and innocent character, and I can swear that she will be second to none; but elevated characters she doesn't understand, doesn't feel, because she has neither the instinct nor the education to sustain them with the nobility and the lofty style they demand. And so, it's my opinion that in *Norma* she will be a nonentity, and that the role of Adalgisa is the only one suited to her character. (Letter of 1 June 1835, Cambi 1943, p. 574)

Nevertheless, in the opinion of many connoisseurs Norma proved to be 'doubtless her grandest performance' (Chorley). Her interpretation was

> modelled on that of Madame Pasta – perhaps, in some points, was an improvement on the model, because there was more of animal passion in it; and this (as in the scene of imperious and abrupt rage which closes the first act) could be driven to extremity without its becoming repulsive; owing to the absence of the slightest coarseness in her personal beauty. There was in it the wild ferocity of the tigress, but a certain frantic charm therewith, which

carried away the hearer – nay, which possibly belongs to the true reading of the character of the Druid Priestess, unfaithful to her vows. (Chorley 1862, vol. I, p. 113)

Grisi's Norma in its prime, in Paris in 1844, was evoked in one of Théophile Gautier's critical essays:

Norma is Giulia Grisi, and never, for sure, did Irminsul have a priestess more lovely or better inspired. She surpasses the ideal. When she makes her entrance, upright and proud in the folds of her tunic, the golden sickle in her hand, a coronet of vervain on her head, her face a mask of pale marble, her black brows and her eyes a greenish blue like that of the sea, an involuntary cry of admiration fills the theatre; what shoulders and what arms! they are surely those that the Venus de Milo lost!

Norma is Giulia Grisi's triumph. No-one who has not seen her in this role can say that he knows her; in it she shows herself to be as great a *tragédienne* as she is perfect a singer. The art of song, passion, beauty, she has everything; suppressed rage, sublime violence, threats and tears, love and anger; never did a woman so pour out her soul in the creation of a role . . .

Giulia Grisi achieves a sublimity in this [opening scene of Act II] which has never been surpassed; truly this is the tragic Muse, the Melpomene of whom Aeschylus and Phidias might have dreamed.[4]

Lilli Lehmann (1848–1929)

Among the great Normas of operatic history Lilli Lehmann was unique in the sense that, for her, Norma was simply one item, no doubt a particularly challenging item, in a huge and astonishingly varied repertory of operatic roles – 170 of them in 119 operas (Pleasants 1967, p. 234) – that extended from Pamina and Donna Anna, via Leonore and Marguerite, Lucia, Lucrezia Borgia and Aida, to Isolde, Sieglinde, Brünnhilde, Fricka and Ortrud. She had been one of the singers that most enchanted Wagner at the first Bayreuth Festival in 1876, when she sang Woglinde, Helmwige and the Woodbird in the first *Ring* cycles; and she was to remain a well-loved recitalist until as late as 1920. She was a great German artist and a great Wagnerian in an age when, among German musicians, Wagnerian music-drama was widely believed to have superseded traditional Italian opera. Yet, not only did her voice retain the charm and flexibility to sing classical and *bel canto* opera; her sensibility and her imagination were generous enough for her to recognize the artistic integrity of a repertory too many German musicians had come to be supercilious about. She, to the contrary, demanded of anyone that presumed to tackle the role of Norma the same kind of high-minded idealism that she brought to Wagner and the classics of the German repertory:

When I think back to that beautiful time [her first Normas in Vienna], and then consider with what lack of knowledge and affection this great opera has subsequently been treated, I must pity the artists who permit such great and rewarding tasks to escape them, as well as the public that thereby loses the lofty enjoyment of a work so rich in melody, the passionate action of which has more human grandeur than many a bungled modern composition that receives great applause. *Norma*, which bears so much love within it, may not be treated indifferently or just polished off. It should be sung and acted with fanatical consecration, rendered by the chorus and orchestra, especially, with artistic reverence, led with authority by the conductor; and to every single quaver should be given the musical tribute that is its due. (Quoted in Porter 1979, p. 166)

The most noteworthy of the evocations of Lehmann's own Norma is Eduard Hanslick's, in a tribute to the great lady written in 1885:

In Italy Rossini, Bellini, Donizetti, often indeed even Verdi, always composed for singers trained in the school of virtuosity, who understood at the same time how to shape a role and how to deliver it dramatically. The abandoning of exclusively virtuoso roles, and indeed of the excessive use of coloratura in opera altogether, is something no-one will complain about; but they might well complain about the extreme state of affairs sanctioned by the newest tendencies, namely that absolutely no real vocal technique is any more demanded from dramatic singers. In the [eighteen-] thirties the best German performers of Donna Anna, Agathe, Euryanthe, Fidelio were at the same time singers trained in coloratura, who didn't miss the chance of roles like Norma.

In Germany today an excellent Norma is the greatest of rarities. Naturally; for our coloratura singers lack the voice and the acting skills, and our 'dramatic' singers lack the vocal technique. For this reason alone it gives us great artistic satisfaction that Lili Lehmann,[5] after her Donna Anna and Fidelio, also sang Norma. She enabled us for the first time in many years to experience the great effects which a voice trained in the school of virtuosity can achieve when it is intimately associated with dramatic powers of acting and passionate expression . . .

[Lili Lehmann's] Norma had the most beautiful portamento in the slow cantilenas, the surest, most delicate attack and swelling on the high notes, a completely pure, fluid coloratura in the decorated passages. The latter never obtruded itself, coquette-like; it remained always noble, serious, subordinate to the context. We may have imagined the thunder of passion still more powerful, the convulsive flashes of jealousy and scorn still more searing – this is an observation that is valid for the climactic moments of all Lili Lehmann's really dramatic roles. I believe that the limitations of her vocal resources are more to blame for that than a certain coolness of temperament, though I wouldn't wish to discount that either. How the effectiveness of a singer or actor is decisively dependent upon the external dowry of nature – far more than on talent, technique or education – that can be observed in Lili Lehmann in a double sense. Since nature denied her a voice of penetrating power or luxuriousness, it excluded the artist from achieving the strongest and most directly passionate effects. On the other hand it gave her, not only a personal letter of recommendation for the stage, but more specifically a commission for all tragic and ideal roles. This tall, slim figure needs only step on to the stage and lift up her head, with its nobly chiselled features and its dark, beautifully set eyes, and one believes without further ado that she is Donna Anna, Norma, Fidelio. And then her flawless poise, her exemplary dress! With her, inspired dramatic nuances always flow spontaneously out of the situation; they never seem contrived, stuck on from outside . . . She is as little prone to the error of over-acting as to that of singing too loudly. In Lili Lehmann the finest artistic education is stronger than the powerful directness of feeling. We do not see her as a powerful force of nature, creating as it were on the spur of the moment; but as a superior spirit which, like polished steel, goes to the heart of every task, finds the treasure and lays it before us free from all dross. (Hanslick 1885)

Something of these qualities may still be enjoyed in some excerpts from the opera – 'Casta Diva' and the duet 'Ah! sì, fa core' (sung in German) – which Lehmann recorded in 1908, when she was fifty-nine. Andrew Porter particularly admires the 'strong, sure tone, noble phrasing, and astounding flexibility. All the runs and ornaments are accurate; she adds two (perfectly formed) trills to the two sustained Cs of the second florid melisma on "senza vel"' [VS 65] (Porter 1979, p. 158).

Rosa Ponselle (1897–1981)

The great Norma of the first half of the twentieth century was the American soprano Rosa Ponselle. Ponselle's relatively brief operatic career (she retired from the stage when she was only forty) began with the most extraordinary of debuts. For having begun to make a name for herself in vaudeville, she came to the notice of Caruso and via him of Giulio Gatti-Casazza, general manager of the Metropolitan Opera in New York, and at the age of twenty-one found herself stepping on to an operatic stage for the first time in her life and singing with Caruso and Giuseppe De Luca as, of all things, Leonora in Verdi's *Forza del destino*. Already she possessed 'a voice of natural beauty that may prove a gold mine; it is vocal gold anyway, with its luscious lower and middle tones, dark, rich and ductile' (James Huneker, quoted in Pleasants 1967, p. 299).

Surprisingly, though Ponselle sang many of the great *verismo* roles, she never tackled Puccini; one of the reasons was surely her almost pathological terror of top Cs. Instead, she and her mentors, particularly Tullio Serafin, perceived in those 'luscious lower and middle tones, dark, rich and ductile' an opportunity to extend her repertory in a rarer way, reclaiming some of the great roles associated with Pasta and her peers a century before. Gatti-Casazza had in fact asked her to prepare 'Casta Diva' for her second Metropolitan audition in 1918. According to a familiar anecdote, she fainted in the middle of her performance; but Gatti-Casazza encouraged her to persevere with the aria 'as a vocalise'. As she herself was later to recall (in the context of some remarks about the exploitation of young singers), her grooming for the great role was infinitely patient.

When Gatti-Casazza, Tullio Serafin, and Romano Romani, my coach, first got together on the idea of my singing Norma one day, they decided I should be ready for it in *five or six years' time*, provided – and this was most important – provided I was given the right roles to lead up to it. After seven years had passed, and I had proved myself by my success in *La Vestale*, I was offered the role of Norma, but that was only after two years of constant preparation on my part. (*Opera: Ponselle 80th birthday issue*, January 1977, p. 23)

Two years later, in November 1927, Ponselle sang her first Norma; the opera had not been heard at the Met. since Lilli Lehmann's 1891–2 performances.

For an account of Ponselle in her prime, however, I cite some recollections of her Covent Garden Norma in 1929.

And then she began to sing. Ponselle invested that first act of *Norma* with a touch of almost divine mystery . . . and when she began 'Casta diva', with a rocklike security of technique and yet a magical beauty of tone, a sort of golden spell reached out and encompassed the whole audience, and it was as though no one drew a breath until the end. Then, contrary to every custom of the period, the whole house erupted in a storm of cheering and clapping. Even the orchestra put down their instruments and applauded.

From then on the evening was hers, the combination of faultless singing and compelling drama lasting until the final notes. After that there was an extraordinary scene, most of us realizing that we had shared in a truly memorable occasion. I remember a man in the amphitheatre throwing his hat into the air (nearly all of us sported hats in those far-off days) crying, 'I've heard every great singer since Destinn, and never one to touch this woman.' (Ida Cooke, *ibid.*, p. 22)

Her dread of top Cs was overcome, partly by transpositions (some of them probably going back to Pasta herself, some seemingly tailor-made for Ponselle), partly by the elimination of cabaletta repeats and much of the flamboyant cadence material that goes with them.[6] These practices had become customary in revivals of the *bel canto* repertory, and were to remain customary down to the time of Callas.

Regrettably there appears to be not much more of Ponselle's Norma on record than there is of Lehmann's. But the aria and the Act II duet suffice to show that its reputation as musically and vocally the most consummate of all was well-deserved. Elisabeth Schwarzkopf tells us that 'the first records my future husband [Walter Legge] played to me were those of Ponselle: "To teach you the meaning of *bel canto*"' (*ibid.*, p. 19). Walter Legge himself tells of a visit he paid to Serafin shortly before the old maestro's death: 'In my long lifetime,' said Serafin, 'there have been three miracles – Caruso, Ponselle and Ruffo. Apart from them there have been several wonderful singers' (*ibid.*, p. 14).

Maria Callas (1923–1977)

One of these wonderful singers was certainly Maria Callas. And, thanks to the long-playing gramophone record, she has come to be more indelibly identified with the role of Norma than was possible for any singer, however great, of an earlier generation. Callas sang her first Norma in Florence in 1948, her last in Paris in 1965. Throughout that period she was supreme in the role. She twice recorded the complete opera and many of her stage performances were also captured on tape; they are therefore vividly remembered; and since they were also uniquely photogenic it has to be said that in the thirty years of productions and recordings since her retirement from the stage no other singer has come even close to challenging her supremacy. To no other of her great roles did she return so frequently or with such a sense of total identification: she sang eighty-nine Normas (compared with sixty-three Violettas, forty-six Lucias, thirty-three Toscas and Aidas, thirty-one Medeas).

Over and over again in these performances she gave audiences that extraordinary sense that musical history was being made in their presence, that this was the kind of occasion they would remember with awe and 'tell our children and grandchildren about' (Harold Rosenthal in *Opera*, March 1957). Franco Zeffirelli, who produced her last *Normas*, at a time when her voice had become a tragic ghost of what it had once been, was still moved to remark, 'In a lifetime, one can see many great things in the theatre, but to see Maria Callas in *Norma*, what is there to compare to it?' (Stassinopoulos 1980, p. 193).

Her ability, even after her voice had begun to fail her, to make *Norma* a supreme musico-dramatic experience for those who heard it has always reminded critics of what was said, 120 years earlier, of Giuditta Pasta herself. Like Pasta's, Callas's voice, at once glorious and intractable, had been tortured into submission by an imperious will and a noble imagination. The ideal Norma, one might suppose, would be one who commands a tireless flow of lustrous tone and a flawless coloratura technique; but experience has proved, from Pasta onwards, that the qualities of a great singing actress are even more vital. Norma must be a mistress of dramatic declamation, who can colour her phrases with an infinite number of shades, and time them and articulate them thrillingly; and she must be an outstanding personality who, simply by her presence and deportment on stage, can rivet an audience's attention. These assets Callas had in abundance, but the role never became less than supremely demanding. 'With Norma,' she said in 1961, having already sung the opera more than seventy times, 'I work as if I had never sung it before. It is the most difficult role in my repertoire; the more you do it the less you want to' (Stassinopoulos 1980, p. 60).

When Callas first studied the role with Tullio Serafin, the conductor who had coached Ponselle in the 1920s and who now became Callas's mentor in the *bel canto* repertory, he told her, 'Go home and come back tomorrow, when I shall want you to declaim the whole opera to me, from start to finish. Not the music, just the words. I know you can *sing* the role, that's why we engaged you. But when you can match the words to Bellini's music, you will find the key to Norma' (quoted in Matheopoulos 1992, p. 179). Her art of declamation was indeed to become thrilling beyond compare. Peter Conrad was inspired by her letter-reading in *Macbeth* and *La traviata* tellingly to redefine Verdi's conception of the *parola scenica*: 'the word which becomes musical when it becomes dramatic, when it turns into the emotion it had previously merely named' (Conrad 1987, p. 318). In later years she may have depended too heavily on the *parola scenica*, but in her prime every vocal resource was at her command, and in a role like Norma she had the uncanny faculty of transmuting everything – the long sustained lyrical phrases, the coloratura, the spasms of what in lesser hands might have seemed mere ornamentation – into something deeply expressive and meaningful.

Dame Joan Sutherland, herself a distinguished Norma, recalled the overwhelming experience of hearing Callas sing 'Casta Diva' for the first time: 'that glorious voice pouring on and on. I remember thinking, "how does the woman *do* it? How does she manage to maintain her voice at such a level and such an intensity?"' (quoted in Matheopoulos 1992, p. 206). John Steane takes her performance of the same aria, compared with that of a number of other great divas, as the starting point for some reflections on what made her performance of the whole role utterly unique, the memory of it indelible as Pasta's had been:

> Callas' distinction in this company is easy to define. Reverting to the simile of the portrait gallery, hers is simply the most interesting and the most fully human face there. Hers is the most aptly expressive treatment of the music: she is rapt but not sleepy, dignified but not statuesque. She sings with what can best be called love; that is, with care, understanding and sudden personal insights, such as a way of dropping the descending chromatic figures from their note with a gentle tone and a soothing suggestion of *glissando* to make an effect like the shining path of moonlight on water. And if this is true of 'Casta diva', it applies still more to the tragic Norma of later scenes. The softly lamenting 'Teneri figli', the baleful sound of the chest voice in 'In mia man alfin tu sei', the tragic shading of the last solo, 'Deh non volerli': these are a few places in which the sound of the music and of Callas' voice become inseparable to one who knows them both. (Steane 1974, p. 378)

What is *Norma* about? As we have seen, for many admirers in the middle decades of the nineteenth century it seemed the very quintessence of the Italianness of Italian opera; the undoubted 'risorgimental' overtones of the dramatic action fitted that interpretation hand in glove. To hear Callas as Norma is to be prompted to a rather different question: who is Norma? One pieces together a response: Norma is priestess and prophetess and wise woman; she is lover and mother, betrayed mistress and avenging fury; she is, as it were, tenderly affectionate elder sister (be it noted that both of what one is inclined to *feel* to be her love-duets are sung not with Pollione but with Adalgisa); she is redemptress and sacrificial victim. The role was designed for the 'encyclopaedic' genius of Pasta, and it is difficult indeed to find in the whole repertory of opera another role that depicts womanhood in so encyclopaedic a fashion. In achieving this, however, Bellini absolutely does not anticipate the more familiar nineteenth-century ideals of womanhood embodied in Verdi's operas. In *Norma* woman is awesome, divine, an enchantress, a figure not of home and hearth but of myth.

There was therefore a sense of inevitable, almost predestined, rightness in the fact that two of Callas's last Normas were sung in the open air in the ancient Greek theatre at Epidaurus. When Lilli Lehmann spoke of performing *Norma* with 'fanatical consecration' she was, though the context was surprising, perhaps doing little more than expressing the typical high-mindedness associated with the late Romantic cult of the holiness of art. Callas's 'fanatical consecration' was something more elemental, atavistic and, if necessary, sacrificial. For years she half starved herself 'in order to sculpt the physique she needed for her characters – for expression, not elegance' (Conrad 1987, p. 322). It wasn't enough 'to have a beautiful voicc; you must take this voice and break it up into a thousand pieces, so she will serve you . . . You set yourself a standard which is always a whip. You're whipping yourself always' (Callas, quoted *ibid.*, pp. 322–3). For Callas, Conrad concludes in his stimulating essay, 'opera was a cult, and entailed a shedding of blood' (*ibid.*, p. 329). In Epidaurus, more than ever before, it became clear why Callas was the supreme Norma: 'here is a woman, in one sense the most modern of women, but there lives in her an ancient woman – strange, mysterious, magical, with terrible inner conflicts' (quoted in Stassinopoulos 1980, p. 255).

The words are those of Pier Paolo Pasolini, and they explain why he felt that Callas's Norma might appropriately lead her on into the world of mythology proper. When her voice had finally been destroyed by twenty years of unsparing self-flagellation, she made her last appearance as a tragic actress in Pasolini's *Medea*, a twentieth-century film recreation of the same fearsome myth that Romani and Bellini had recreated so magnificently for their own Romantic age.

APPENDIX I

Borrowings

Bellini draws upon four earlier compositions for *Norma*. In chronological order they are:

1. *Adelson e Salvini* (1825)
The cabaletta of the Act I duet between Salvini and Bonifacio includes, towards its close, an animated new theme on the words 'con questo mano il core saprò dal sen strappar' (ex. A1). This was adapted and reworked in imitative form at a similar juncture in the Act II duet for Norma and Adalgisa, at the words 'Teco del fato all'onte' (VS 182).

2. *Bianca e Fernando* (second version, 1828)
This provided material for two movements:

(i) Bianca's *aria di sortita* has a cabaletta, 'Contenta appien quest'alma', which is reproduced almost in its entirety, though with its coloratura somewhat chastened, to serve as the cabaletta of Norma's *sortita*, 'Ah! bello a me ritorna' (VS 73).

(ii) The Act II chorus 'Tutti siam' provides the material for the Act II chorus in *Norma*, 'Non parti?' (VS 188). In this case the borrowing came via a third opera, *Zaira*, where the same material had been used for the chorus of French knights mourning the death of Lusignano, 'Poni il fedel tuo martire'. Bellini's contemporary, Federico Ricci, was in no doubt that the movement reflected Bellini's familiarity with Beethoven's C♯ minor Sonata, Op. 27/2 (MS letter, Naples Conservatory Library).

3. 'Bella Nice, che d'amore', composed sometime between 1827 and 1829, and published as No. 3 of *Sei ariette per camera* in 1829 by both Ricordi in Milan and Giraud in Naples, provides the material for that part of the Adalgisa/Pollione duet beginning 'Sol promessa al Dio tu fosti' (VS 96).

Ex. A1

4. *Ernani* (1830)

Material from the opera abandoned in the late autumn of 1830 was employed in both *La sonnambula* and *Norma*. The *Norma* reworkings are as follows:

(i) The *Andante* of the Elvira/Ernani duet 'Muto e deserto speco' supplied the principal theme for the *Andante* of the Act I finale, 'Oh! di qual sei tu vittima' (VS 136).

(ii) 'Meco regna', an *Andante* designed for an Elvira/Carlo duet in *Ernani*, became the aria 'Ah! del Tebro' sung by Oroveso in Act II of *Norma* (VS 199). In this case Bellini had already tried to incorporate the material in the Adalgisa/Pollione duet.

It is not usually easy to suggest at what stage or for exactly what purposes Bellini decided to have recourse to pre-existent material. The following points are, however, suggestive:

(i) Several examples entail near identity of sentiment: 'Ah! bello a me ritorna'; 'Non partì?'.

(ii) Several examples entail formal or structural parallels: 'Teco del fato all'onte' (coda of duet cabaletta); 'Oh! di qual sei tu vittima' (part of a complex movement in which a duet turns into a trio); 'Non partì?' (placed at the darkest moment of the opera before the final denouement).

(iii) 'Bella Nice' might be a case of desperation. On the evidence of the sketches, Bellini resorted to this only after hours and hours of work trying to get the Adalgisa/Pollione duet into a shape that satisfied him.

APPENDIX II

The tonal plan of 'Norma'

Sinfonia	G minor/major

Act I, Scene 1: The sacred forest of the druids

No. 1 Coro d'Introduzione e Cavatina (Oroveso)

Coro	G major
Cavatina	G major

No. 2 Recitativo e Cavatina (Pollione)

Recitativo	C minor → V of C major
Cantabile	C major
Tempo di mezzo	E♭ major
Cabaletta	E♭ major

No. 3 Coro – Scena e Cavatina (Norma)

(a) Coro	E♭ major

(b) Scena e Cavatina (Norma)

Scena	E♭ major → V of D♭ major
Cantabile	G major
Tempo di mezzo	E♭ major → V of D minor
Cabaletta	F major

No. 4 Scena e Duetto (Adalgisa, Pollione)

[Prelude]	B♭ major
Scena	B♭ major → D♭ major → (implied) V of A minor
Tempo d'attacco/ Cantabile	F minor/A♭ major
Tempo di mezzo	A♭ major → V of F minor
Cabaletta	A♭ major

Notes: The *cantabile* of No. 2 was originally composed in B♭ major.

The *cantabile* of No. 3(b) was transposed to F major, apparently for Pasta herself, and most editions of the opera print it in that key. There does seem an anomaly in consequence, though, for it is surely most unlikely that Bellini would have prepared a *cantabile* in G major with a recitative closing in D♭. The first version of the scene envisaged a cabaletta in A♭ major.

The whole of the mistletoe ceremony scene is contained within a tonal orbit of G, C, and E♭ major.

The tonal scheme of No. 4 was one of many aspects of the number that underwent considerable revision during composition. So numerous were the changes of mind that it is difficult to be quite sure which group of revisions belong with which; but it appears that Bellini's original tonal layout may have been more simply conceived, the Prelude being sketched in C major, the remainder in A♭ minor/major.

Act I, Scene 2: Norma's dwelling place

No. 5 Finale

(a) Scena e Duetto (Norma, Adalgisa)

[Prelude]	A minor
Scena	A minor → B♭ minor
Scena *a due*	B♭ major → V of F major
Cantabile	F minor/major
Tempo di mezzo	→ V of C major
Cabaletta	C major

(b) Scena e Terzetto (Norma, Adalgisa, Pollione)

Scena	C major (with digressions) → V of B♭
Cantabile	B♭ major
Tempo di mezzo	E♭ major → V of G minor
Stretta	G minor/major

Notes: A violent shift of key marks the change of scene.

Though the finale itself lacks overall tonal coherence, its two constituent parts are organized by perfectly straightforward tonal progressions:

A minor [F] → C major in the duet
[C] B♭ major → G minor/major in the trio.

The autograph shows that the original tonal layout of the trio entailed an A major *cantabile*, followed by a D♭ → A♭ minor/major *tempo di mezzo* and stretta.

The act as a whole is tonally closed in G.

Adalgisa's B♭ links up with that in Scene 1; she is also the 'subject' of the B♭ *cantabile* in the trio. While the fact is striking, it is also the case that two of these occurrences of B♭ are the result of second thoughts.

Act II, Scene 1: Inside Norma's dwelling place

No. 6 Scena e Duetto

(a) Scena (Norma)

[Prelude]	D minor
Scena	D minor → V of B♭ major

(b) Scena e Duetto (Norma, Adalgisa)

Scena	B♭ major → (implied) V of C major
Primo tempo	C major
Tempo di mezzo	C major → V of F major
Cantabile	F major
Tempo di mezzo	→ V of F major
Cabaletta	F major

Notes: This is a clear example of a large-scale scene with an unbroken musical continuity describing a simple progression from minor to relative major key (cf. both parts of the Act I finale).

Adalgisa is again introduced in B♭ major.

Act II, Scene 2: A lonely place close to the druids' forest

No. 7 Coro e Sortita (Oroveso)

[Prelude]	F major/minor
Coro	F minor/major
Recitativo	F major → C major
Aria	F major

Notes: Surprisingly, there is no change of key to mark the change of scene; that fact is not attributable to any association between F major and the druidic music in Act I.

Act II, Scene 3: The temple of Irminsul

No. 8 Finale

(a) Scena e Coro

[Prelude]	C major
Scena	C major → V of A minor
Coro	A minor/major

(b) Scena e Duetto (Norma, Pollione)

Scena	C major → E minor/G major → V of F major
Cantabile	F major
Tempo di mezzo	F minor → D♭ major → V of A♭ major
Cabaletta	A♭ major

(c) Scena ed Aria Finale (Norma)

Scena	A♭ major → V of G major
Cantabile	G major
Tempo di mezzo	C major → V of E minor
Stretta	E minor/major/minor

Notes: The layout of the whole finale is dominated by mediant relationships – C/A; F/A♭; G/E – within an overall C/E. The apparently violent A♭ to G move in section (c) is achieved via an enharmonic A♭/E shift which anticipates the closing tonality.

APPENDIX III

Liszt's 'Réminiscences de Norma'

There follows a fuller account of the Liszt work briefly described in Chapter 7.

The 'Réminiscences' are best conceived as falling into three linked movements:

I [Introduction and first movement: key centre G]

i. (bars 1–27) *Tempo giusto* G minor

An introduction: the chosen key is that of Bellini's *Sinfonia* but the material is that that accompanies the assembling of the Gauls for the mistletoe ceremony. Startling is the evocation of an Italian operatic *tutti* in four-part *ff* chords in the centre of the keyboard, almost as if Liszt were really trying to suggest the 'red-hot lump of metal' that Tovey liked to evoke in describing the brass writing in Verdi's early scoring. Note too that Bellini's timpani are replaced by quasi-side-drum (i.e. more military-sounding) rolls. In the third phrase Liszt changes Bellini's harmony to introduce diminished sevenths; these then dominate the fourth phrase, cast in the form of high spread (bardic?) chords. The music breaks down into a freely composed, cadenza-like link, making striking use of chromatic colour.

ii. (bars 28–88) *Quasi andante* G major etc.

This begins as a straight, though very rich, transcription of the introductory processional music from the *Coro d'Introduzione* – both its scene-setting music and its *banda* march. It is initially the pianistic colour of the transcription that is so arresting. Not content with simply reproducing Bellini's orchestral texture, Liszt thickens and darkens it, doubling each strand at the lower octave, and turning the throbbing pedal note into harp-like fifths, octaves and twelfths. He adds an additional chromatic nuance, where Bellini had already shown the way, at 38.

Liszt's recomposing really takes off towards the end of the repeated phrase, as the original material becomes conventionally transitional. He limits himself initially to little bravura touches, projecting the triplets of the accompaniment figuration of 41f. through the 'sighs' of 47–8, thus loosening the metrical rigidity, and linking the trilled pedal notes at 49–54 with coruscating scale passages. The *banda*-accompanied theme appears in its due place at 56, but is more freely treated than anything heard yet, with chordal thickening and touches of imitation. At 60, the point where Bellini begins to – as it were – position Oroveso for his 'Ite sul colle', a moving bass line emerges, and Liszt uses this to support a series of modulations against which the theme is developed. From 66, B major (anticipating the next major division of the structure) becomes the key centre and the march theme is restated in a more lyrically pianistic form. From 75 to 82 rich broken chord patterns take over (B, g♯, E♭, c, G); there is vague comparability here with the mediant juxtapositions in Bellini's scene (at VS 21–2), but the actual choice of chords is Liszt's own. What is most striking here is his use of this rich wash of sound to float a rhythmic motif ♩ 𝄿♬ ♪ 𝄾 ♪ 𝄾 which makes explicit the thematic/rhythmic link between the druids' procession and the chorus 'Dell'aura tua profetica'.

iii. (bars 89–145) *Allegro deciso* G major

A transcription of 'Dell'aura tua profetica' as far as the coda (= VS 22.1.3). The link into the theme and into the return of the chorus at Fig. 15 is flamboyantly expanded, and the keyboard idioms are furiously massive and virtuosic. They change with (though hardly to reflect faithfully) Bellini's changes: solo voice at 101, soft dynamics with trombone chords at 109. There are additional chromatic nuances at 116, and Liszt 'improves' Bellini's chromatics at 127 (D for d) and 128 (c for C). Essentially all this is faithful to the original until it is suddenly snapped off at 145 with a reprise of the opening bars a semitone higher and massively retextured.

iv. (bars 145–70) Transition

Some third of the way through Liszt's paraphrase, we have heard nothing but Gaulish warrior/druid music. The only section whose semantic purport is unmistakable is the warlike prophecy of the overthrow of Roman imperial power. This transition announces the voice of the individual in the form of a recitative. This continues the ♪. ♬ ♩ ♩ rhythm of the previous processional and warlike music, punctuating it at first with ghostly memories of the invocatory chords of (i). But the harmonies become richer, the recitative inflections more pathetic, and we find that what Liszt's transition is also doing, besides simply linking the public and private spheres, is demonstrating their thematic affinity. For the rhythmic motif apparently separated out from the march music proves also to be the principal thematic idea of 'Deh! non volerli vittime', which is to be the starting point of the *cantabile* section of the work.

II [Slow movement: key centre B]

It is surely correct that Lisztian reminiscences of a Bellini opera should culminate in a mood of ecstatic lyricism. That goal is arrived at with formidable sophistication in two waves: the first (171–238) is the more sustained, and draws on three sources:

v. (bars 171–90) *Andante con agitazione* — B minor
A transcription of 'Deh! non volerli vittime', unextended and undeveloped.

vi. (bars 190–219) *Più lento* — B major
A transcription, subsequently extended and developed, of 'Qual cor tradisti'.

vii. (bars 220–38) *Più lento* (continued) — B major
A transcription of 'Piange, prega'.

(v) 'Deh! non volerli vittime': as the melody becomes more passionate Liszt treats it in more freely pianistic style, progressively thickening the texture. What is most striking is surely the highlighting, the drawing to our attention, of what is actually there in Bellini's (often despised) accompaniment: the pizzicato bass, the syncopated horn, the lurching string figuration; by thickening up the latter he actually draws attention to the quiddity of Bellini's orchestral texture.

(vi) 'Qual cor tradisti': the accompaniment is dissolved into a richly pulsing 12/8. The thrilling timpani that stand out so startlingly from the naive see-sawing of Bellini's original scoring are no less conspicuous here, recast rhythmically to fill the melodic interstices with poetic substance, and the melody is thickened out in thirds and octaves (as happens in Bellini's choral coda). With these provisos it is faithfully transcribed as far as 198. In the central section of the melody, at 198, 200, 202, where Bellini's harmonic progressions verge on the rustic, Liszt makes them smoother, more urbane, more chromatic. Instead of leading the melody on to its reprise/culmination, he then uses a cadenza/coloratura link to dovetail into, as it were, the answering verse, which is set in the manner of a variation, making the melody more continuous (in readiness for section (vii)) and setting it beneath high reiterated chords, like those woodwind flutterings that in Italian opera so often symbolize unearthly ecstasies. At 214 the same dovetailing process happens again, and at 215 Liszt begins a further variation over a clattering octave bass. This time, after an oddly balanced five-bar phrase, it culminates in a bravura full close. The repetitions, the growing richness, the combination of lulling and ecstatic sensuousness, the sense of infinite reserves of rhetorical virtuosity barely held in check, are all justly observed elements of Bellini's operatic language.

(vii) 'Piange, prega': the gorgeousness of (vi) leads into a transcription of the passage Lippmann has often compared with Wagner's *Liebestod* for its sheer intoxicating sonority. Here the melody is set out in plain 4/4 in the midst of washes of broken chords. Note that the opening two-bar phrase is played twice not thrice: after (vi) Liszt already has a well-established grand *maggiore* base from which to launch the chromatic sequences of the climax. Note too that to maximize the sonority he keeps his chords in root position until the very last moment (229) rather than imitating Bellini's chromatically rising bass. A varied repetition is cut short at 239.

viii. (bars 239–48) *Tempestuoso* Modulating

A freely composed transition, though it anticipates the principal motif of 'Guerra, guerra', leading into:

III [March-Scherzo and Finale-Apotheosis: key centre E♭]

ix. (bars 249–330) *Doppio movimento: Presto con furia* E♭ minor

A transcription of the *Coro di guerra* in the form of a series of variations on the principal thematic material, and without reference to the *maggiore* conclusion. For this we move to the final principal key centre E♭: these mediant relationships – g/G; b/B e♭/E♭ – are another Italianate (though also of course another Lisztian) feature of this extraordinary paraphrase. Liszt transcribes it as far as VS 216 (Fig. 38), and then composes two variations on the same material. Given the repetitiousness of Bellini's chorus this has the effect of being a transcription of virtually the whole piece as far as VS 219 (bottom line). In reducing 272 to single notes (like the opening bars, this is one of the places where Liszt's version is simpler than the VS) he again draws attention to an odd feature in the original – an ominous tumbling in the silence. The brilliant feature of the transcription is the inner animation of the chunky chords and the intensification of their *martellato* aggressiveness by the bravura use of hand alternation, cross-rhythmed and later trans-octaved. By variation two (299–320), this is becoming a scherzo-like movement, the sounds of warfare dissolving into a firework display. The lamest of transitions accelerates into:

x. (bars 331–59) *Meno allegro* E♭ major

The all-engulfing love-music of Bellini's finale returns to conclude the work. Here Liszt does use Bellini's threefold statement of the opening two-bar phrase to launch it (of course in intensifying variation rather than mere repetition). The theme is surrounded at first by cascading scales, but from 337 the arpeggios resume their sway, now in a rather different form that allows for, indeed makes a characteristic detail of, the chromatically rising bass: the texture simplifies further into harp-like spread chords at the climax.

The repetition (345f.) (two statements only of the opening two-bar phrase) is pianistically more straightforward, but poetically denser, because it incorporates as countermelody the opening figure of the bellicose druid chant 'Dell'aura tua profetica', variously recast to fit the harmony. At the climax Liszt returns to the same material as at 343, but this time, by a simple turning back on itself, it is drawn out to twice its length, before a diminished seventh chord cuts short its impassioned ecstasies.

xi. (bars 359–71) Coda E♭ major

A brief cadential coda, triumphant rather than, as in the opera, tragic.

Notes

1 The composition of the opera

1 In achieving a fee of 12,000 Austrian lire = 10,400 francs Bellini, for the first time in Italian operatic history, 'broke through the 10,000-franc barrier and established a new record' (Rosselli 1996, p. 72).
2 Mercadante was in Turin preparing the premiere of *I Normanni a Parigi*.
3 This is one of the letters that is preserved only in Florimo's version; it may have been touched up by him.
4 Tintori, for one, is unimpressed by this point of view (1983, pp. 167–8).
5 The first, the letter in which Bellini invites her comments on the subject, and requests her assistance in acquiring figurines of the characters as they appeared in Soumet's tragedy, has already been quoted.
6 The letter is quoted in Chapter 9.
7 The grand ballet would be performed between the two acts of the opera; the lighter ballet at the end of the evening.
8 Among the performers, making his last run of appearances after a tenure of close on thirty years as *maestro al cembalo* at La Scala, was Vincenzo Lavigna, best known to musical history as Verdi's teacher (Phillips-Matz 1993, p. 46).
9 Such at least is the traditional account. However, the letter in which, immediately after the performance on 26 December, Bellini describes the evening to Florimo does not appear to survive. Florimo reports that he gave the original to Lord Palmerston's brother, 'cavaliere Temple', who was then Minister of Her Britannic Majesty at Naples (Weinstock 1992, p. 489). Cambi conjectures that in transcribing it for publication Florimo will have 'retouched and prettified it' (Cambi 1943, p. 290).
10 Pacini's mistress, Countess Giulia Samoyloff.

2 Medea – Velleda – Norma: Romani's sources

1 In their 'Avvertimento' the Italian authors explain that they have found Noël unreliable on the classics and have therefore rewritten those articles completely. But in 'the articles on Nordic and Asiatic mythology . . . [they found him] a reliable guide, perhaps preferable to all others', and only occasionally amplified or revised his work. A system of asterisks makes it possible to see where they have done that.

2 Or indeed to grubbily tendentious purpose; for whatever one's views on the phenomenon of Napoleon, it is surely dismaying that so fine a spirit as Heinrich von Kleist could ever have imagined his *Hermannsschlacht* to be edifying.

3 Synopsis and musical frame

1 Brennus, a chieftain of the Sennonian Gauls, defeated the Romans at the Battle of the Allia in 390 BC and sacked Rome. To him is attributed the phrase 'Vae victis'.

2 By the 1880s it had become customary to perform the opera as a four-act work, the second act beginning here (D'Arcais 1882, p. 812).

4 Music and poetry

1 See the critics quoted by Maguire 1989, pp. 184–5.

2 The number includes the second, Genoa, version of *Bianca e Fernando*.

3 NB The Celts counted the passing of time by nights, not days; see Piggott 1968, p. 116.

4 Cf., however, Rosselli 1984, pp. 165–6, and 1996, p. 101; he is deeply sceptical about any 'risorgimental' overtones.

5 Erasmi 1988–9, p. 98: early in 1831, stimulated by the July Revolution in Paris, a series of patriotic revolts had occurred in Modena, Bologna and Parma.

6 I use X^v to mean that X is repeated, but varied and at a higher pitch.

7 There is some evidence in the libretto drafts that Romani may have intended a further lyrical movement, which would help explain the long 'codetta': for if one is reading this evidence aright the 'codetta' was in fact conceived as a *tempo di mezzo*.

8 Bellini in fact requested from Romani 'eight lines of prayer' at this juncture (Branca 1882, p. 170; Scherillo 1882, p. 85). Romani was evidently not disposed to oblige and Bellini took matters into his own hands.

9 See, however, under AL in Chapter 5.

10 In his autograph score Bellini himself provided a simplified Violin 1 part for the *tempo d'attacco*; it is a poor thing compared with the original.

11 The first chorus words, 'Norma! che fu?' etc. are sung to a variant of the chordal progression heard at the beginning of No. 3.

12 *Rima baciata* is the type of rhyme that falls into an a.a.b.b. etc. pattern (Elwert 1968, p. 101).

5 A glimpse of the genesis of the opera

1 One highlights the conspicuous use of *decasillabi* in this scene because of the associations the metre had acquired during the Romantic period, thanks particularly to Manzoni. Giovanni Pascoli, in an article in Battaglia's *Grande dizionario della lingua italiana*, speaks of the 'galloping *decasillabi* . . . which accompanied the legions on their marches and consoled the sorrows of the exiles' (Quoted in Engelhardt 1988, p. 19).

2 There is much conjecture in my reading of this *tutti*. (NB I do not believe that 'Tutti ah! tutti' can be anything other than an aria text, and therefore could not have been intended to be followed by 'Ah! riedi ancor', as Branca suggests. Its a.b.b.c;a.d.d.c. rhyme-scheme is exactly that Romani is most fond of in closed numbers.)
3 A key signature of four flats must be added: the accidentals by which Monterosso tries to put it into A minor can then be dispensed with.

6 Some variant readings

1 Bellini himself seems to have been in two minds. In the autograph score he first marks the cut ('*taglio al segno*'), then later cancels it ('*si fa*').
2 In this diagram, b b′ x are the subdivisions of the phrase B, c c′ y z the subdivisions of the phrase C, etc.; b b′ and c c′ show that the phrases are in part made up of symmetrical repetitions, x y z that they are in part made up of non-recurring continuations.
3 The piano solo issued by Ricordi, plate nos. 5775–5786 (cf. Lippmann 1969, p. 386) included only the more extensive close.
4 The 'sketches' CAT 42–41 show that the *maggiore* coda was composed *before* the music of the body of the chorus.

7 Contemporary reactions to *Norma*

1 Cf. Boito's 'Letter to Broglio', extracts from which are conveniently available in Walker, *The man Verdi*, London 1962, pp. 461–2.

8 Critical fortunes since the Unification of Italy

1 I have been unable to trace in the Bizet literature the source for Cecil Gray's story of Bizet's attempting to reorchestrate *Norma* and giving up in despair. Is this one of the charming fictional *trouvailles* that enliven Gray's writings, or is 'Bizet' in this case a fusion of dimly-remembered tales of Chopin and Wagner?

9 Five prima donnas: contributions to a performance history

1 An excerpt from her *Norma* embellishments is quoted in Garcia's *Traité complet de l'art du chant*, Paris 1840.
2 The C, D, E at the top of the treble stave according to Adelaide Kemble, who for a time studied with Pasta (Christiansen 1984, p. 68).
3 Chorley's comment on her roulades brings to mind a tribute from Ferdinand Hiller: 'When Pasta . . . began "Oh non tremare, o perfido", and hurled her scale-passages at Pollione, no Shakespearean poetry could have been more deeply affecting' (Hiller 1880, p. 151).
4 It was during Grisi's reign that a first major transformation took place in the manner in which the opera was staged. The original La Scala production had sets designed by Alessandro Sanquirico which, despite the opera's setting amid the barbarian tribes of ancient Gaul, employed the

massive neo-classical, architectural style for which he was renowned (see plate 2). But in northern Europe the early nineteenth century was a period of intense archaeological interest in druids. The first English edition of *Norma*, published by Boosey in 1848 incorporates 'an account of Bellini's Norma' by 'J. W. M.', which includes a huge amount of information about the druids, and reports that a first production to be influenced by these archaeological findings had been staged by the English Opera Company at Covent Garden in 1841; Adelaide Kemble was the Norma. By the end of the decade, with the spread of the railways and the beginnings of operatic touring in Britain, we find Benjamin Lumley, the impresario, and his Italian opera company disporting themselves at Stonehenge, 'where Sontag sang "Casta Diva", and Lablache a portion of Oroveso's music among the Druidical remains, so suggestive of the opera of *Norma*' (*The Mapleson memoirs, 1848–1888* (2nd edn), London 1888, vol. I, p. 3).

5 Hanslick's spelling.
6 See Ardoin 1976 for details.

Bibliography

Abbreviations

AnMc	*Analecta musicologica*
JAMS	*Journal of the American Musicological Society*
ML	*Music and Letters*
NOHM	*The New Oxford History of Music*

Atti del convegno internazionale di studi belliniani 1985. Catania.
L'Avant-scène/Opéra 1980. Special *Norma* number, Paris, September–October.
La revue musicale 1939. Special centenary number, May.

Adamo, M. R. and Lippmann, F. 1981. *Vincenzo Bellini*, Turin.
Alajmo, R. (ed.) 1986. *I teatri di Vincenzo Bellini*, Palermo.
Andò, C., De Meo, D. and Failla, S. E. 1988. *Bellini, mostra di oggetti e documenti . . . Catalogo*, Catania.
Ardoin, J. 1976. 'A footnote to Ponselle's Norma', *Opera*, March.
1977. *The Callas legacy*, London.
Baldacci, L. 1974. *Libretti d'opera e altri saggi*, Florence.
Beffort, A. 1908. *Alexandre Soumet: sa vie et ses œuvres*, Luxembourg.
Berlioz, H. n.d. 'Bellini: Notes nécrologiques', in *Les musiciens et la musique*, Paris.
1836. 'Bellini', *Journal des Débats*, 16 July.
Black, J. N. 1988. 'The libretti of Felice Romani: a bibliographical survey', in *Felice Romani*, Moneglia.
1992. 'Romani, Felice', in *The New Grove Dictionary of Opera*, London & New York.
Branca, E. 1882. *Felice Romani ed i più riputati maestri di musica del suo tempo*, Turin/Florence/Rome.
Brauner, C. S. 1976. 'Textual problems in Bellini's "Norma" and "Beatrice di Tenda"', *JAMS*, 29.
Budden, J. 1981. *The operas of Verdi*, vol. III, London.
Cagli, B. 1971. 'Vincenzo Bellini', in *Guida all'opera*, Milan.
Cambi, L. 1943. *Vincenzo Bellini: epistolario*, Milan.
1973. 'Bellini: un pacchetto di autografi', in *Scritti in onore di Luigi Ronga*, Milan.

Cella, F. 1968. 'Indagini sulle fonti francesi dei libretti di Vincenzo Bellini', in *Contributi dell'Istituto di filologia moderna dell'Università cattolica del S. Cuore*, V, Milan.

Celletti, R. 1969. 'Il vocalismo italiano da Rossini a Donizetti. Parte II: Bellini e Donizetti', *AnMc*, 7.

Cescatti, O. (ed.) 1994. *Tutti i libretti di Bellini*, Milan.

Chorley, H. F. 1862. *Thirty years' musical recollections* (2 vols.), London.

Christiansen, R. 1984. *Prima donna: a history*, London.

Conrad, P. 1987. *A story of love and death: the meaning of opera*, London.

D'Arcais, F. 1882. 'La "Norma" di Bellini', *Nuova antologia*, December.

Dean, W. 1982. 'Italian opera', in *NOHM, vol. VIII: the age of Beethoven*, London.

Deathridge, J. 1988. 'Reminiscences of "Norma", in *Das musikalische Kunstwerk: Festschrift Carl Dahlhaus* (ed. H. Danuser), Laaber.

de La Grange, H.-L. 1973. *Mahler*, vol. I, New York.

Elwert, W. Th. 1968. *Italienische Metrik*, Munich.

Engelhardt, M. 1988. *Die Chöre in den frühen Opern Giuseppe Verdis*, Tutzing.

Erasmi, G. 1988–9. '*Norma* ed *Aida*. Momenti estremi della concezione romantica', *Studi verdiani*, 5, Parma.

Florimo, F. 1880–4. *La scuola musicale di Napoli e i suoi Conservatori* (4 vols.), Naples.

Gatti, C. 1964. *Il teatro alla Scala* (with *Cronologia completa degli spettacoli e dei concerti*, ed. G. Tintori), Milan.

Gautier, T. 1945. 'Norma', in *Les beautés de l'Opéra*, Paris (also in *Souvenirs* 1883).

Gray, C. 1926. 'Vincenzo Bellini', *ML*, 7.

Hanslick, E. 1888. 'Lili Lehmann' (1885), in *Musikalisches Skizzenbuch: (Die moderne Oper IV)*, Berlin.

Hiller, F. 1880. *Künstlerleben*, Cologne.

Joly, J. n.d. '"Oltre ogni umana idea": le mythe, la tragédie, l'opéra dans la "Norma" de Bellini', in *Nos ancêtres les Gaulois. Actes du colloque international de Clermont-Ferrand* (ed. P. Viallaneix and J. Ehrard), Clermont-Ferrand.

Lichtenthal, P. 1826. *Dizionario e biografia della musica*, Milan.

Lippmann, F. 1967. "Quellenkundliche Anmerkungen zu einigen Opern Vincenzo Bellinis', *AnMc*, 4.

1969. 'Vincenzo Bellini und die italienische Opera seria seiner Zeit', *AnMc*, 6.

1973. 'Ein neu entdecktes Autograph Richard Wagners: Rezension der Königsberger *Norma*-Aufführung von 1837', in *Musicae scientiae collectanea: Festschrift Karl Gustav Fellerer*, Cologne.

1977. 'Belliniana', in *Il melodramma italiano dell'ottocento. Studi e ricerche per Massimo Mila*, Turin.

1982. 'Wagner e l'Italia', in *Wagner in Italia* (ed. G. Rostirolla), Turin.

1990. 'Lo stile belliniano in "Norma"', in *Opera & Libretto I* (ed. G. Folena *et al.*), Florence.

Mack Smith, D. 1968. *A history of Sicily: modern Sicily after 1713*, London.

Maguire, S. 1989. *Vincenzo Bellini and the aesthetics of early nineteenth-century Italian opera*, New York and London.
Mariano, E. 1990. 'Felice Romani e il melodramma', in *Opera & Libretto I* (ed. G. Folena *et al.*), Florence.
Matheopoulos, H. 1992. *Diva*, London.
Monterosso, R. 1973. 'Per un'edizione di "Norma"', in *Scritti in onore di Luigi Ronga*, Milan.
Morini, N. 1918. 'La *Norma* e le meticulosità di un revisore', *L'archiginnasio*, 13, Bologna.
Neri, C. (ed.) 1991. *Lettere di Vincenzo Bellini (1819–1835)*, Palermo.
Pastura, F. 1959a. *Vincenzo Bellini*, Catania.
1959b. *Bellini secondo la storia*, Parma.
Phillips-Matz, M. J. 1993. *Verdi: a biography*, Oxford.
Pieri, M. 1994. 'Trentaquattro piccoli film più uno per Vincenzo Salvatore Carmelo Francesco Bellini', in Cescatti (ed.).
Piggott, S. 1968. *The druids*, London.
Pizzetti, I. n.d. 'La musica di Vincenzo Bellini' (1915), in *La musica italiana dell'ottocento*, Turin.
1940. *Vincenzo Bellini*, Milan.
Pleasants, H. 1967. *The great singers*, London.
Porter, A. 1979. 'Norma', in A. Blyth (ed.) *Opera on record*, London.
Pozzoli, G., Romani, F. and Peracchi, A. 1809–25. *Dizionario d'ogni mitologia e antichità, incominciato da Girolamo Pozzoli sulle tracce del Dizionario della favola di Fr. Noel, continuato ed ampliato dal Prof. Felice Romani e dal Dr. Antonio Peracchi*... (6 vols.), Milan.
Regli, F. 1865. *Elogio al Felice Romani*, Turin.
Rinaldi, M. 1965. *Felice Romani: dal melodramma classico al melodramma romantico*, Rome.
Rinuccini, G. B. 1843. *Sulla musica e sulla poesia melodrammatica italiana*, Lucca.
Ristori, A. 1888. *Studies and memoirs*, London.
Ritorni, C. 1841. *Ammaestramenti alla composizione di ogni poema e d'ogni opera appartenente alla musica*, Milan.
Roccatagliati, A. 1990. 'Libretti d'opera: testi autonomi o testi d'uso', *Quaderni del Dipartimento di linguistica e letteratura comparato*, 6, Bergamo.
1996. *Felice Romani librettista*, Lucca.
Rosselli, J. 1984. *The opera industry in Italy from Cimarosa to Verdi*, Cambridge.
1996. *The life of Bellini*, Cambridge.
Rovani, G. 1859. *Cento anni*, Milan.
1874. 'Bellini', in *Le tre arti considerate in alcuni illustri Italiani contemporanei* (2 vols.), Milan.
Scherillo, M. n.d. *Belliniana. Nuove note*, Milan.
1882. *Vincenzo Bellini: note aneddotiche e critiche*, Ancona.
1892. 'La "Norma" di Bellini e la "Velleda" di Chateaubriand', *Nuova antologia*, June.
1920. *'L'Arminio' di Pindemonte e la poesia bardita*, Messina.

Schlitzer, F. 1954. *Mondo teatrale dell'ottocento*, Naples.
Stassinopoulos, A. 1980. *Maria: beyond the Callas legend*, London.
Steane, J. B. 1974. *The grand tradition: seventy years of singing on record*, New York.
Tari, A. 1911. 'Vincenzo Bellini', in *Saggi di estetica e metafisica* (ed. B. Croce), Bari.
Tintori, G. 1983. *Bellini*, Milan.
Torrefranca, F. 1934. *Il mio Bellini*, Rome.
Wagner, R. 1983a. 'Pasticcio von Canto Spianato' (1834), in *Richard Wagner: Dichtungen und Schriften*, vol. V (ed. D. Borchmeyer), Frankfurt.
1983b. 'Bellini. Ein Wort zu seiner Zeit' (1837), in *Richard Wagner: Dichtungen und Schriften*, vol. V (ed. D. Borchmeyer), Frankfurt
Weinstock, H. 1972. *Vincenzo Bellini: his life and his operas*, London.

Index